IMPACT!

Deliver Presentations That Get Results

Marjorie Brody
Speaker Hall of Fame, Professional Certified Coach

IMPACT!

Copy Editors: Leslie Miller, Miryam S. Roddy & Heather Shafter
Cover Design: Justin Sloan
Copyright 2015 by Marjorie Brody & Career Skills Press

Printed in the USA.
ISBN 978-1-931148-57-3

Acknowledgments

Writing a book continues to be a group effort. There are so many people who have contributed. My special thanks go to the following:

Miryam S. Roddy, who acted as a project manager and chief copy editor.

Leslie Miller, who took my initial words and ideas and organized them so they made sense.

Heather Shafter, for reviewing my material, and offering fresh insights and useful tweaks in many areas.

Justin Sloan, who developed graphics and the cover.

The BRODY team of trainers, for their insights and ideas. Colleagues, clients and friends who read the material, and were eager to write book testimonials.

BRODY clients for their continued support and providing the content for each chapter – whether it's modeling the behaviors that I'm describing or continually raising the bar to improve their presentation skills.

More Testimonials for *IMPACT!*

Mark Sanborn, bestselling author of *The Fred Factor* and *You Don't Need a Title to be a Leader*: "If you want to speak with impact, this book will give you the tools and techniques you need to get the results you desire. Marjorie Brody is a true pro that writes from experience and you will benefit from her ideas and insights. I recommend it."

Alan Weiss, Ph.D., author, *Million Dollar Consulting* and *The Consulting Bible*: "Marjorie Brody is the High Priestess of presentations and provides the royal road to high impact."

Brian Tracy, speaker (5000+ presentations) and author (70 books): "This is a terrific book, written by one of the top speaking professionals in America today, telling you exactly what you can do, from the first word, to give powerful, influential talks and presentations."

Ruby Newell-Legner, Certified Speaking Professional, President of National Speakers Association, 2015-2016: "One key skill that can make a career flourish or flounder is how you communicate. Marjorie Brody has created a practical guide filled with tools, techniques and loads of experience to teach you positive ways to deliver presentations. Follow her blueprint to achieve your next promotion and take hold of your future!"

Jennifer Zinn, Vice President, Strategic Affairs, Roche Diagnostics: "Brody delivers again! This puts the power in the presenter's hands -- a one-stop shop for delivering presentations that MATTER."

Shep Hyken, *New York Times*-bestselling author of *The Amazement Revolution* & president National Speakers Association: "There are three words that will guarantee a successful presentation: preparation, preparation and preparation. And your first step to prepare is to read this book."

More Testimonials for *IMPACT!*

Ron Karr, author, *Lead, Sell or Get Out of the Way* & Past President of National Speakers Association: "This book shows you how to make a killer presentation and get what you want. If you are willing to do what it takes and follow the strategies in this book, you will be unstoppable when it comes to presenting your ideas and gaining acceptance."

Lisa Ford, author of best-selling training series, *How to Give Exceptional Customer Service*: "This is a book that every business presenter needs to read. The ideas go from basic to advanced, and they are easy to understand and apply."

Brian Lee, Certified Speaking Professional and President, Custom Learning: "The world has a few 'must have' invaluable tools for all communicators in search of an exceptional presentation. I am in awe of the quality, usability, and value of this superb 'how-to' book on presentation excellence."

Terri Kabachnick, CSP – author, *I Quit But Forgot To Tell You;* CEO & Founder, the Kabachnick Group, Inc. and an International Executive/Leadership Coach and Professional Speaker: "If you want to succeed in speaking – whether you are a professional speaker or want to improve and expand your presentation skills in a corporate environment -- write these words with a magic marker on your brain: 'Remember, the success of any presentation lies with changing your focus from being self-driven to your audience members and their needs.' These are only some of the golden nuggets that you'll find in Marjorie's latest book. As a professional speaker, I have listened to Marjorie's words of wisdom for over 20 years. She knows what makes an audience love you and respond to you. Read this book, then read it again, and then put into action what she tells you to do. Your success as a speaker and presenter will follow."

Art Sobczak, sales trainer, author of *Smart Calling* and President of Business By Phone: "Your success in business and life is proportionate to your ability to communicate and

More Testimonials for *IMPACT!*

persuade. In *IMPACT!* Marjorie shows you precisely how to present like a pro, regardless of whether you do it every day, or are scared silly to speak to a group. Get it, use it, and you will love your results!"

Dr. Alan R. Zimmerman, best-selling author, CPAE Speaker Hall of Fame: "Few things will impact your career more quickly and more positively than your ability to deliver exciting and engaging presentations. And no one teaches you how to do that better than Marjorie Brody. Indeed, hundreds of thousands of people can trace the success of their careers to the presentation skills she taught them. It's time that you count yourself among her loyal and grateful followers. Read this book, read it now, and you'll be thrilled with the results you get."

Randy Gage, author of *The New York Times* bestseller, *Risky Is the New Safe*: "Brody knows exactly how to make a major impact. If you want to influence, inspire and also impact – this is the book to read."

Bill Lee, Lee Resources, Inc., Greenville, SC: "In her latest book, *IMPACT! Deliver Presentations that Get Results,* Marjorie Brody hits it out of the park. Anyone who thinks they are great presenters needs to read this book. I make presentations for a living and I found myself wishing I had read Brody's new book a long time ago."

David Newman, Certified Speaking Professional, author of *Do It! Marketing*: "Marjorie Brody nails everything you need to know -- and DO -- to present like a pro in this masterful book. If you want to maximize your influence, impact, and income, you need to become the most powerful messenger of your message. Whether you're an executive, entrepreneur, or independent professional, you will find valuable step-by-step strategies, a few insider secrets that few professionals even know, and a host of smart 'do-this-now' tips that will make you stand out every time you get up to speak."

IMPACT!

TABLE OF CONTENTS

Introduction

Although flip charts gave way over time to PowerPoint slides, and notes on paper gave way to notes on iPads, the actual art of speaking is, has always been -- and will always be -- about communication between human beings.

While the importance of genuine communication between people hasn't changed, the fact is that the ongoing technology revolution has dramatically changed people's attention spans.

According to the website StatisticBrain.com, the average American's attention span in 2013 was shorter than a goldfish's! In 2000, the average attention span was only 12 seconds -- not very long at all. By 2013, it had shrunk by a *third,* down to eight seconds. I bet it's even less now!

What does this mean for those of us who give presentations? After all, any presentation we'll ever have to give will be longer — much longer — than eight measly seconds. Even TED Talks are 18 minutes.

People are increasingly overwhelmed with external stimulation of all kinds. Multi-tasking is rampant and smart phones are the perfect distraction. Whether you give formal, work-related presentations or speak at meetings, you've probably already noticed how many people are often surreptitiously checking their phones or texting, even while you speak.

The question becomes, how do you capture an audience's attention and hold it long enough to get your points across and/or call them to action? What kinds of things truly engage an audience so that they will stay with you, focused, attentive, and absorbing your message? How can you create impact?

While the principles of giving an effective, moving, persuasive, or eye-opening presentation are largely unchanged — what *has* changed is the outright necessity of mastering those principles. Your material must be relevant and compelling from the first sentence because modern business audiences will not cut you any slack ... not even eight seconds' worth!

Once upon a time, you might have gotten by with the following presentation opening: "Hi, I'm John Disorganization from the Irrelevant Company. I'm so happy to have the opportunity to be speaking to you fine people today. It's amazing that I am even standing here now to tell you about it, because the traffic on the interstate was so bad. My talk will be on why digital technology is just a fad, and analog communication is definitely here to stay."

Yep, you might have gotten by with that opening back in the old, pre-Twitter and pre-smart phone days (although I'd never recommend starting a presentation that way). Your audience might have still been awake and listening when you finally segued into something relevant. But you certainly will not get by using this approach in our current fast-paced, on-to-the-next-item-of-business mentality, where snap decisions are made the minute you open your mouth.

Business presentations must be well-thought out, expertly organized, and individually adapted to the medium you're using, your audience and its needs, and the time frame available. This holds true whether you are giving a presentation to senior management, a keynote at a conference, or even an impromptu conversation with others during a team meeting.

With some careful planning and practice, you can deliver presentations that have your audience fully attentive and engaged. You can learn to give presentations that enhance your career by showing you as a thought leader -- dialogues that leave your audience inspired and persuaded to take action ... talks that change peoples' minds and affect their business decisions.

Whatever your purpose for giving a presentation, you can achieve it by following the guidelines and time-tested best practices in this book. Learn the foundations of outstanding presentations for every type of business situation.

This book is divided into sections – starting with the basics – putting a presentation together, how to get started, what to include, and how to organize.

The second section delves deeper into various types of presentations, including persuasive presenting, speaking virtually, and presenting to senior management.

The final sections deal with delivery dynamics, delivery styles and handling questions.

But, I don't want to challenge your attention span any further with this introduction, so let's get right to it!

Author's comment:
Warning! This book is primarily for people who give business presentations – though the approach and techniques are similar for all presentations. I use a variety of examples – not only from business. If the example doesn't resonate with you, just replace it with your own. The principles will still apply.

Chapter 1

The Preparation Process:
Start Presentations With Your PAL™

"Prior and proper planning, preparation and practice prevent poor performance." ~Marjorie Brody

If you approach presentations with a survival mentality, only wanting to get them over with as painlessly as possible, you are missing a phenomenal opportunity to bolster your career.

Creating a powerful and memorable presentation might be more work, but it will lift you far above the rest. You can greatly enhance your reputation, open many new doors, or even show yourself as a thought leader in your area of expertise.

So, rather than just trying to survive a presentation, why not raise the bar?

Of course, knowing your subject matter inside out is an absolute must, but that's just the beginning. The key to nailing any kind of presentation is preparation, plain and simple.

If you have some type of professional presentation coming up, here's the first thing you should **not** do: create a slide show.

Technology *should not* be the foundation of your presentation. Remember, it's only an aid to your presentation. Instead, go analog – unplug! Think about what you want to achieve.

To prepare for an effective presentation, try this approach that we've been teaching at BRODY for more than 30 years with great success. It continues to stand the test of time: **Analyze Your PAL™** (**P**urpose, **A**udience, and **L**ogistics).

Knowing your PAL™ can take you from an anxious, tech-dependent speaker to a more confident, audience-centered speaker. Remember, the success of any presentation lies with keeping your focus on your audience members and their needs. Here's what it's all about:

"P" is for Purpose

Business presentations usually fall into one of two types: informational and persuasive. Your first step is to decide your ultimate purpose and outcome. Of course, there will be some overlap, but decide which of the three is the main focus of your presentation. Everything you create for your presentation — your words, your slides, your anecdotes, your facts -- should fall in line with your purpose.

1. The Informative Speech

Main purpose: sharing information with others.

If you are in business, many of the presentations you will give will be the informative kind. Informative presentations include sales reports, project updates, research data, analysis of competitive products, or training.

Your material must be interesting enough to capture an audience's attention and keep it focused. Remember, the amount of information retained decreases as your presentation continues. To make the most powerful impact, counteract this natural human tendency to lose focus by:

- making your material as interesting and relevant as possible (no droning on and on with one fact after the next)
- reinforcing your key ideas throughout the presentation (strategic repetition)
- organizing your information in a logical way that makes sense to your audience
- incorporating visual aids like photos, graphs, charts (seeing is not just believing, it's also the way many people learn best).

- engaging audience members with stories, humor, anecdotes and examples (keeps them awake and entertained)
- using a strong opening that will get their attention, show the value of listening to you and establish yourself as a credible source
- preparing a strong ending, which includes summarizing your key points in a way that will be easy for your audience to remember

By carefully preparing your presentation in advance, you ensure your audience retains as much information as possible.

2. The Persuasive Presentation

Politicians, salespeople and leaders -- at least the good ones -- are the masters of this type of presentation, used to influence audience members or motivate them to a certain action. Successful business speakers also use these same "emotion plus logic" techniques to enhance their credibility with the audience.

Other situations for a persuasive presentation may include:
- persuading prospective clients to choose your company
- persuading employees to accept changes
- persuading management/school board/etc. to approve and fund a project
- persuading your manager to promote you or give you a raise
- persuading a valuable potential employee to join your firm

Presentation Tip
Levels of persuasion:
- **Convince –** attitudinally, the audience supports your point of view.
- **Actions –** the audience takes the necessary action. They do what you ask, i.e. vote, buy, or approve a project.

In order to be persuaded, the audience members first must be informed and motivated. If you want them to take action, they must be attitudinally aligned with what you are asking.

Aristotle said all speaking is persuasive speaking, because you are "selling" your own credibility along with your ideas. The word "persuasion" might have negative connotations for you. If so, you aren't alone. Many people make judgments on politicians and their ability to "persuade" others by promising the moon — but never delivering it. Other people are uncomfortable with salespeople's ability to persuade others to purchase things they don't need or want. And yet, there may be times you'll be called upon to give a persuasive speech about something you believe in or care deeply about. You'll need to put those preconceptions and prejudices aside, and learn to persuade others in an authentic yet effective way. I'll address this in later chapters.

It's rare at work to have a need to deliver a purely entertaining presentation. If you want to keep your audience members involved, however, using elements of entertainment for your informative and persuasive presentations is effective.

Now that you have established what type of speech you're giving, move on to the "A" in PAL™ .

"A" is for Audience

Another presentation skills book that I wrote was called *Speaking is an Audience-Centered Sport.* Why? Because the focus of all presentations needs to be the audience. After all, you are giving the presentation to inform, to sway opinion, to enlighten, to offer true benefit to your listeners.

Consider your audience members -- their skill level, whether they are your peers or laymen, their familiarity with your subject matter, and their possible perspectives. Do you know what attitudes they might already hold about your topic? Are they in line with what you'll be presenting, or will you be trying to win them over to your point of view?

The more you can customize your presentation to the needs of your audience members (always keeping your own purpose in mind) the better they will assimilate the information, remain responsive, and give your presentation high marks for value.

If audience members aren't interested in your topic, find an angle that will engage them. There is usually something in it for them. If you are speaking within your company or industry, you'll probably be able to judge whether an audience will be hostile or receptive, depending on the topic. If it's about upcoming bonuses (and it's good news), you're in luck. If it's downsizing, you may have a difficult time.

When you can choose a topic yourself, knowing who comprises the audience will let you select a subject that interests as many members as possible. Misjudging your audience, or not knowing who the members are, can have disastrous effects on even the best-executed presentation. Knowing your audience will help *put you in control*. And the feeling of control will greatly enhance your confidence.

Presentation Tip: The time it takes you to prepare an audience profile may mean the difference between success and failure for your presentation.

The best source for information about your audience will be the program organizer or person who asked you to make the presentation. For more information, you can also:
- Talk to people who will be in the audience
- Do research on the Internet
- Talk to others who have presented to this group before.
- Speak to administrative assistants
- Get annual reports or promotional materials to help you learn more about the group
- Read literature about the company and any information pertaining to its corporate culture

Developing an Audience Profile

What do you want to know – and need to know – about your audience members before beginning to create your presentation?

When developing your own audience profile, include the following categories:
- demographics
- psychographics
- attitudes
- decision-makers
- learning styles

1. Demographic Profile: This includes audience characteristics such as age, education, occupation, socioeconomic group, and marital status. These factors can affect your choice of words, the information you choose to include, illustrations and examples, and humor if you are including any. The more details you have about your audience, the less risk there is of offending anyone, speaking over their heads, boring them, or including too much or too little information.

When developing an audience profile, include as many of the following demographics as you can, if they are relevant:
- Male/female ratio

- Age range
- Technical/non-technical
- Education levels
- Where they live/work
- Marital status

Knowing about any of these demographics can better inform you as to what should be included in your presentation. For instance, if the audience for your presentation is all 20-somethings, you might prepare very different anecdotes than if it spans WWII vets to Millennials. If your audience has a technical background, you can be much more technical in your presentation than if the audience will consist of laymen without an understanding of your subject matter.

2. Psychographic Profile

This includes what you can learn beforehand about their *feelings and impressions on your topic*. Again, the program organizer is your first line of information. A psychographic profile should include the following data:

- What do they think about your topic? Is it new to them?
- Have they attended any presentations on similar topics?
- What are their hopes, aspirations, dreams, goals?
- What are their interests?
- Why are they attending the presentation?
- Do they want to be there?
- Are they politically active?
- Have they supported causes like yours before?
- Are they open-minded?

3. Attitudes

Know your audience members' attitudes before you start planning. What are their attitudes toward what you propose – exactly what are their objections and concerns?

Here are five types of audiences that you will face:

- **Favorable –** We love them! All favorable audiences are rare. They are yours to lose.

- **Uninformed –** They came with a blank slate. Your job is to give them information that will help them.

- **Apathetic –** They just don't care. Here, you'll need to emphasize the WIIFM? (What's In It For Them?)

- **Hostile –** You will often encounter hostile audience members when giving a persuasive presentation. It's critical to understand the source of the hostility, so you're prepared to counter it. If they don't like or respect you, the chances of success are limited.

- **Mixed –** Of course, the mixed audience which includes several of the different types of attitudes are the hardest. I go into more detail about this in Chapter 3.

4. Decision Makers

Capturing a positive reaction from decision makers in attendance can make your presentation a success even if others in the audience disagree. Knowing if decision makers will be in the audience will help you target your remarks.

When presenting within your own company, consider:
- Will there be people from many departments with different agendas, or will you be speaking to a narrower base?
- Will you be speaking to employees at your own level, or from different levels?
- Is the company president going to be there, your immediate supervisor, or someone you are trying to influence?

> **Presentation Pitfall:** Avoid addressing your comments only to one or two decision-makers in the audience. This could backfire by making you look like a "teacher's pet" and by making the rest of the audience feel less important. In addition, take into account the people who influence the decision-makers. Their opinions count, too.

5. Learning Styles

If possible, also consider the learning styles of your audience members. By understanding these styles (visual, auditory, and kinetic), you will be able to decide the best way to present your information.

So, the more you know about your audience, the more precisely targeted a presentation you can make. The more precisely targeted, the greater chance your presentation will be an overwhelming success!

The biggest mistake speakers make is not really knowing their audience. A great presentation to the wrong audience will get no results! Spend time getting to know your audience.

Public Speeches

When delivering a public speech, there is a whole different set of requirements. The wider the range in your audience, the more difficult it is to tailor your presentation to meet everyone's needs.

If you will be speaking in something other than a business situation, it becomes even more difficult to analyze the audience members.

- Why are they part of the audience (why are they there)?
- Are they all residents of the same town?
- Do they all attend the same church, synagogue or mosque?
- Are they all the parents of teenagers?

- Are they all interested in the same issue (hopefully the one you are speaking on)?
- What are their expectations and goals?

Establishing a common bond with your audience members will be easier once you know more about them. Spend the time up front; it is well worth the effort.

And, for the third part of PAL™ ...

"L" is for Logistics

The savvy presenter always factors in logistical considerations. When determining logistics, find out the following:

- How much time do you have?
- How many people are in the audience? (Important if you are providing handouts)
- What time will you be presenting? (If your presentation is right after lunch, people might be a bit sleepy and able to afford you less concentration than they otherwise could. Knowing this, you will want to make your presentation more interactive and less slide-driven.)
- If there are other presenters, where are you in the lineup? (People's ability to absorb more information might fade as the day goes by. If you are on late in the day after a full program, you may need to be more dynamic, attention-grabbing, and interactive.)
- Who speaks before you? After you? What are they speaking about? (Knowing this will help you create a presentation that does not offer the exact same material.)
- How much time will each speaker have?
- What happens if a speaker runs over his or her allotted time limits?
- How long will there be for questions and answers?
- Will the Q & A be held at the end of each speaker's portion, or will they be taken at the very end?
- Where, exactly, will you be presenting? What is the

size of the room and how will it be set up?
- What equipment is available? Is a microphone provided or must you bring your own? Is there WIFI? A screen? What AV capabilities does the venue have?
- How is the room arranged?
- How formal or informal is the organization you're speaking to? (It's good to know this so you'll dress appropriately and feel more confident.)

Write a Central Theme

Once you have analyzed your PAL™, write one sentence that answers the question, "What do you want that audience to know, to do, or to feel as a result of this presentation?"

Remember ...
"A theme is a memory aid; it helps you through the presentation just as it also provides the thread of continuity for your audience." ~~ Dave Carey

If you're having trouble focusing on the theme, try this exercise:

Imagine that after your presentation, someone who did not attend asks one of your audience members, "What was it all about?" What would the answer be? If you have trouble writing your presentation, it's because you weren't clear about the outcome you wanted.

Chapter 2

Crafting a Successful, Targeted Presentation, Step by Step

Each different type of presentation -- from a virtual meeting to an important report for senior management -- has its own best practices. There are general strategies, however, for developing a cohesive presentation that will work for any situation.

You've already done your PAL™ analysis and written your central theme. Now it's time to begin developing the presentation.

There's a strategy behind crafting a compelling presentation. Before you create any slides, you need to know what information you want to include, and how to present it most effectively.

Begin by going analog.

Brainstorm First, Organize Second

Let your creativity flow and start brainstorming. Consider writing each idea on an individual "sticky note" and slapping it on a whiteboard or desktop. It's easy to move them around and organize them, allowing your most effective presentation to take shape right in front of your eyes.

Whether you use a notebook or computer, in this stage you're looking for a rich supply of possibilities from which to compose your presentation — but of course, you will not wind up using all of them. Don't summarily reject an idea because it seems too outrageous. It might lead to an even better idea, or you might realize that a touch of the outrageous is just what you need to capture the attention of those sleepy, presentation-weary audiences.

"Sticky notes" on a white board not your style? Check out these different software/apps for brainstorming and organizing your ideas.

- **Prezi:** http://prezi.com/. This next-generation, cloud-based app allows visual mind-mapping and has what they call "a zoomable user interface" (ZUI) that lets you hone in on certain ideas, so you can better demonstrate your thought process. Customize your presentation from scratch or choose from various, easy-to-work-with templates.

- **The Brain:** http://www.thebrain.com/. Designed for mind mapping, this free software helps you make sense of the wide range of information you'll need to organize for your presentation.

- **AllMyNotes Organizer:** http://allmynotes.vladonai.com/. A tool for organizing notes, project management, presentations, and more.

- **Google Presentations:** http://www.google.com/drive/. Also free and cloud-based, this Google offering is fantastic if you are developing a presentation with others.

After brainstorming what you already know about the topic, move on to using outside data and research. All information should be current, relevant, and *correct.*

Go Beyond Facts & Figures

For the most part, presenters are quick to include data – facts and figures. Yes, presentations need to have these. Yet, data typically isn't what makes a presentation "sticky." Look for opportunities to include engaging content and interactive techniques.

Here are a number of ideas:

- **Short anecdotes and examples:** Great for bonding with an audience, but as always — remember your purpose and the audience's needs. Don't ever ramble on about yourself. If you've got a story to tell, make sure it ties in to the theme of your presentation. For example, if your topic is stricter controls in airline baggage handling, you might use your own trials and tribulations as a business traveler waiting for checked sample cases only to receive them opened and with missing items.

- **Stories:** People tend to remember stories — that's why they are so powerful. But you don't want someone to remember the story but not your main message, so make sure that the two are strongly related. Use witty, heartwarming, startling or even alarming stories to illustrate any of your main points. Integrate them smoothly into your talk: "Let me tell you about my first call on a major client." Storytelling is so important to a successful presentation, that I have a whole chapter about it coming up.

- **Unique audio/visual aids:** These make the experience more of a multi-sensory event. We are all multi-sensory creatures, some of us are primarily visual learners, some audio, some tactile. The more of the five senses that you can include in your presentation, the greater your chances of keeping everyone engaged and learning. Visual aids also allow your audience members to "see" places or things they might not know of, and they can be used to bring statistics to life. Of course, most business presentations will be supported by slideware. More and more presentations are including video clips to add variety and bring a message to life.

  To illustrate misleading packaging, you might show two cans of tuna, both exactly the same size, but with differing weights. By reading the labels and showing the cans to audience members, they will be able to see as well as hear your point.

- **Quotations:** Give you the chance to add an expert's opinion to back up your own, and make great attention-getters. People love quotes. Make sure yours relate to the point you are trying to get across, or are memorable in some way. "As our company founder always said: The customer is everything."

- **Comparisons:** These can provide similarities, and contrasts provide differences. Use them to help audience members relate what they already know to what you want them to know.

- **Statistics:** Useful to support your own theories or disprove others. If you are trying to get your neighbors to support a community watch program, show statistics which demonstrate the reduction in crime for city blocks with community patrolling vs. streets without patrols. But use statistics with discretion. Facts and statistics alone often become data dumps -- not the most interesting or memorable way to share information.

Presentation Pitfall: The Internet is loaded with information that might have been accurate at the time it was posted, but could now be completely out of date. Many websites do not date their posts. And there is an enormous amount of inaccurate information floating around the web. Be very careful which sites you draw your facts from, to make sure that they are, indeed, facts. Nothing will sink your presentation and destroy your credibility faster than stating "facts" that turn out to be erroneous.

- **Rhetorical questions:** These are questions asked by the presenter, with no answer expected from the audience. They are used to persuade, invite the audience to agree with you, or get your listeners thinking. An example of a thought-provoking rhetorical question might be, "How are you sabotaging your career goals?" Some examples of the persuasive type of rhetorical questions could be, "Given how hard you've been working — don't you deserve to be recognized for your contributions?"

"Now that you have all the facts comparing the two systems, can you see how this will improve productivity?" Or, "Isn't this the direction we've always wanted to take this company?"

- **Analogies/Similes/Metaphors:** Analogies are a tool to help people understand new things. They work by creating a link to what they already know: "The building was designed to bend like a tree in high winds." Similes are figures of speech that compare one thing to another to create a very descriptive visual image in the listener's mind: "sharp as a tack." A metaphor is a word or phrase that compares two people, things, animals, or places: "John is a walking dictionary."

- **Humor:** According to Bob Orben, former director of the White House Speech Writing Department, "Business executives and political leaders have embraced humor because humor works. Humor has gone from being an admirable part of a leader's character to a mandatory one." Humor is not the same as telling jokes. Don't tell jokes, unless you are speaking at a comedy club. Also, make sure your humor is not offensive, or hurtful in any way. Consider your audience. Not everyone will get the same jokes or topical references.

My top reasons to incorporate humor in your presentations:

- It helps you connect with your audience.

- It makes you more likable and overcomes any disadvantage from an overly flattering introduction. And of course, the more audience members like you, the more likely they are to be open to and agree with your ideas.
- It keeps audience members' attention — and keeps them awake. Unfortunately, attention spans are

becoming shorter and shorter. We need to deliver a well-put-together, fast-paced program that will quickly capture and keep their attention. Humor integrated in various places helps you do this.

- It causes laughter, which releases endorphins. When that happens, not only will you feel good, it also helps the audience to feel the same.

- It helps emphasize your points and ideas. Humor can be the very nail that hits your audience members on the head with your points and drives them home.

- It disarms hostility. Use non-frivolous humor to take the hostile edge off an audience that is clearly against you.

- It reduces status. This is a bigger deal than you might think. If you are one of the senior leaders of your organization, your very position may create a big barrier to listening. A little self-effacing humor can go a long way toward knocking yourself off your own pedestal and making your audience more able to hear you.

- It gets your points across without creating hostility, and lightens heavy material. Sometimes you have to deliver tough negative messages. The careful use of humor can help you deliver your message without having your listeners wanting to shoot the messenger.

- It helps audiences relate to facts and figures. Spice them up with a touch of humor — perhaps even humor about how dry and deadly facts and figures can be. Joan Eisenstodt, a former MPI Meeting Planner of the Year, says, "High content, informational speakers almost always fall flat if they don't use some humor. I equate appropriate humor with warmth, and audiences respond to warmth."

- It creates a positive bond and shows that you don't take yourself too seriously. If you can laugh a little bit at yourself at the right times, your audience can laugh *with* you and not *at* you.

- It paints pictures in the audience's minds, making information more memorable. In Professor Joyce Saltman's doctoral dissertation, *Humor in Adult Learning,* she concluded, "Most researchers agreed that humor generally aided in the retention of materials as well as to the enjoyment of the presentation of the information."

Look for an emotional connection

The more you can connect with your audience members, the more sympathetic and open they'll be to your ideas. This is one of the basic elements of persuasion.

Interesting stories help make your presentation memorable! People respond first to emotion, then justify it with logic. So provoke an emotional connection first, then add in all the facts and figures.

In a presentation on home fire safety, you might mention published stories of what's happened in area homes when smoke detectors were not installed or not working. In a presentation on building a skateboard park, you could mention a community member's child who was badly injured by a car while skateboarding in the street.

Emotional appeals: *"By approving this, patients will have access to the drugs they need ..." "Let's bring our talents together and take this company to the leading edge of ..."* Don't forget, fear works as an emotion too. *"We can't afford to wait for our competitors to bring this to market first! It's time to..."* More on the topic of persuasion appears in Chapter 7.

Audience involvement: One way to involve your audience is to ask questions.

"How many of you have struggled with influencing your managers?"

"Who is interested in getting techniques to influence without authority?"

"Today I will give you three techniques which will help you influence up, sideways and down."

Other ways to involve your audience members: using their names, asking rhetorical and real questions; using their examples; having them do something. Modern audiences like to participate – look for ways to involve them.

Look for places where others can contribute. Jot down places in your presentation where you might ask for a show of hands, ask questions of the audience, etc. "I'd like to go around the table and hear your opinions." More on the topic of facilitative presenting appears in Chapter 8.

All of these different components enrich a message, making it more memorable — and keep audiences engaged. The idea is to avoid the dreaded information dump, where someone simply talks at a crowd, droning on and on with one dreary bit of information after the next.

The more you can break it up, the more you can introduce stories or examples, the more you can involve your audience (where appropriate), the more your message will be understood, absorbed, and appreciated.

Presentation Tip: Keep idea files – physically or electronically. Whenever you find a newspaper, magazine, journal or web-based article, or hear something you would like to remember, put it into this idea file. Don't trust your memory. I was once told a story that was so incredible, I wanted to use it in a seminar I was leading later that week. I didn't write it down, because I was sure I would remember it. The day of the seminar, I went blank on the story and couldn't tell it to the class. What a missed opportunity! That night, I called the person who told me the story, asked her to please repeat it, and wrote it down. I'm using that story in my presentations to this very day.

Key Takeaways

- Brainstorm and research all possible materials to include in your presentation (manually or electronically).
- Along with facts and figures, be sure to include the following:
  - ✓ Stories and examples
  - ✓ Analogies and metaphors
  - ✓ Quotes and humor (when appropriate)
  - ✓ Audience involvement
- It's a combination of logic and emotion that engage and move an audience.

Pitfall to Avoid: Presenting other people's theories as facts can get you in hot water and cause your audience to question your credibility.

Chapter 3

Organization Techniques that Deliver

"Organizing is what you do before you do something, so that when you do it, it is not all mixed up." – A.A. Milne, renowned author of Winnie-the-Pooh books.

You've researched, you've brainstormed – now it's time to organize all the materials you collected.

There are many different ways to organize your presentation, depending on your goals, purposes, audience, and subject matter. A well-organized presentation acts as a road-map for your audience, leading them from one point to the next and dropping them off at the exact destination you intend.

As productivity expert Scott Belsky says, *"An idea can only become a reality once it is broken down into organized, actionable elements."*

Ready to Organize Your Material?

Here are some tips:
- Cluster your ideas into *three to five main points* for the body of your talk. Research suggests most people tend not to retain more than three points, so make them count.
- Never present your information as a dry, boring laundry list of items. There's no faster way to put an audience to sleep.
- Create an outline. Always. Without fail.
- Consider your material in terms of "must know," "should know," "could know." If you have the time, include it all. If not, you'll know which is the most important information to include and what you can eliminate. Don't leave "must know" information until the end; you'll be kicking yourself if your time is cut short.

Outlines are a terrific tool for creating the most effective presentation you possibly can. Some people love outlining, others loathe it—but regardless of how you feel about the outlining process, a professional quality presentation requires that you do it. It helps you to create the flow in a logical manner.

Let's see if we can't make the outlining process a bit more painless.

The *phrase outline* is the most popular method. To use it, you'll jot down phrases or bullet points that are just long enough to remind you of what you want to say. You'll be able to glance down at your outline, and know exactly what you need to say. (And this is why I am going to keep stressing the necessity of practice and more practice throughout this book!)

You may wonder what the problem is if you're writing out full sentences and paragraphs containing every thought. Well, you're likely to start reading every word, which is fine when using a teleprompter, but otherwise it will blow the spontaneous feeling you're going for and take your attention off the audience for way too long. Unless your presentation is a book reading—don't just read your notes.

Some exceptions to the "no reading rule" would be when quotes, statistics or other facts must be presented precisely. In this case, it's perfectly acceptable to use your notes or slides.

Transitions

These are the statements used between your main points, the review of your main points, and your final, memorable statement.

Transitions refocus your audience's attention, let you repeat your main points without sounding redundant (very important), and help move the listener from point to point. Examples of transitions: "another way to look at," "along with," "we have just covered," "let's move on to the next point" and "the second point is."

A presentation should be telling a story – it needs to be easy to follow and well-constructed. Here are many methods to organize informative presentations:

Organization of the Informative Speech

The informative speech can be organized many different ways, depending on topic:

1. Chronological order. Terrific for showing changes over time. You might use a time line to illustrate the process. Visual aids can be effective in demonstrating the time span to your audience.

For example, if your company is involved with rail transportation, you might create a presentation based around this fact from the American Public Transportation Association: The American public took 10.7 billion trips during 2013, the second highest ridership in 57 years. Since 1995, public transit ridership is up 37.2 percent and is continuing to grow.

You would emphasize this growing trend with all the pertinent data at hand, but you could also show a timeline or graph, dramatically illustrating the rise (and fall, in certain years) of public transportation and how it's affected your industry, your particular company, and what it forecasts for the future.

You can also use "where we were, where we are, and where we are going." This is a great approach for describing projects.

2. Spatial/Geographical order. These presentations pertain to the nature of space (not the "final frontier" kind; the kind that deals with the layout of a room, the blueprint for a new facility, etc.). Spatial order presentations work best when combined with visual aids, so the audience can see what you are talking about.

For example: If your presentation involves movie theaters' treatment of patrons in wheelchairs, visuals showing the layouts of different theaters will help your audience visualize the best (and worst) seating arrangements for these patrons.

3. Topical order. This type of presentation takes a large topic and subdivides it.

For example: You're speaking of private and public schooling. Private schools could be further divided by parochial, same sex schools, boarding schools, and day schools. Public schools could be broken down by inner city vs. suburban and rural. This method works well for discussing a variety of products.

4. Cause and effect. Start with what has happened, or what will happen, and then explain what the results will be. You also can give multiple scenarios and conclusions using the cause-and-effect format.

For example: if your company now allows job sharing for some employees but not others, you may wind up with disgruntled employees, risk lawsuits, and end with an unproductive work force.

5. What? So What? Now What? This is a blend of the informative and persuasive models. So often, speakers spend much of their time sharing how they got their information, the work they did, the time they spent, when for the most part, audiences don't need to hear it and start to tune out. Don't lose them right at the beginning.

Instead of spending so much time on the "What?" give a quick synopsis of what's already been done and then move into the "So What?" phase. "So What?" takes the gathered results and information and connects the dots. It gives insights as opposed to just data.

The "Now What?" phase is where you suggest what you can do with these insights, what recommendations you are suggesting.

For example, your company asked you to investigate the benefits of starting an internship program through local universities. You've compiled your data and are ready to present your findings.

In the **What?** phase, instead of relaying every conversation you had with senior management about starting the project, how you determined which universities to reach out to and which faculty to speak to, which other companies you spoke to about their internship programs, how long the research took, how many pages of data you've compiled, ad nauseam, merely begin your presentation explaining your task and what the purpose of it was. You can always provide more details if the audience asks for them.

In the **So What?** phase, you extract the important information from the **"What?"** and create insights, making the important findings and what they mean obvious to the audience. You'll present the information you gathered, state your case for whether you believe internships would benefit your company, give the reasons behind your conclusions, and offer any statistics or relevant facts you've learned that support your points and your conclusions.

Finally, the **"Now What?"** You've done the work, and get the necessary information. You've done your audience analysis and have formulated ideas. Now it's time to make recommendations based on all you have done … "Based on our findings, I (we) recommend that we move forward with an internship program and start planning for it as soon as possible."

This can be a bold move, depending on the situation. It certainly will set you apart from most people who are strictly data collectors giving a report. Is it worth the risk? Only you can decide!

Informative Presentation Planning Sheet

SPEECH PLANNING WORKSHEET —— INFORMATIVE

Central Theme:

Consider: Purpose, Audience, and Logistics (PAL™)

Main Point:	Main Point:	Main Point:
Supporting Data:	Supporting Data:	Supporting Data:

Transition → Transition →

Introduction 10-15%

Grabber: Source Credibility:

W.I.I.F.T.?:   Preview:

Conclusion 5-10%

Review:

Memorable Statement:

© 2014/2015 (BRODY 215.886.1688 • BrodyPro.com
Professional Development

Informing an audience is also necessary when the end goal is to persuade them. This approach, however, needs to be more strategic.

Approaching the Persuasive Presentation

If you need to persuade an audience, the difference between success and failure may rest on your ability to know your audience's attitude before organizing your presentation. This was already discussed in Chapter 1, but it is important enough to reinforce.

Basically there are five types of audience attitudes:

Favorable: You are preaching to the choir, people who already share your opinions and probably want the same things you want. It's rare to get an entirely favorable audience; if you do, your task will be much easier. Of course, you always want to reinforce their thinking and give even more motivation for action.

For example: You are presenting a proposal for free, on-site day care to staff who currently must find it off-site. They will be a highly receptive audience.

Uninformed: They are neither for nor opposed to what you have to say—in fact they know nothing about it. Your job is to educate them, using facts and arguments that will sway them to your opinion.

Apathetic: This audience couldn't care less what you have to say, usually employees who are required to attend your talk, training, or presentation. Get through to them by showing exactly how they'll benefit from whatever you are proposing. (WIIFM? again!) Create the need!

Hostile: Although no one wants a hostile audience, it's better to know going in so you can prepare. What is the source of their hostility? What are their issues: time, expense, philosophy, you and what you represent, etc.?

Mixed: There are two types of mixed audiences: the favorable mix and the hostile mix. The favorable mix includes favorable, uninformed, and apathetic members. You'll have to inform the uniformed and convince the apathetic there's a genuine need or real benefit to them.

Warning: If even one audience member expresses hostility, the entire audience can shift quickly to his point of view. At this point, you are dealing with a hostile mix. Your challenge? Disarm the hostile members and win them over as soon as possible.

If you are prepared for a hostile audience, *you will be ready for any mixed group.*

It is up to you to determine and address the reasons for any hostility. Take heart, in most cases it has nothing to do with you personally. Budget cuts, pending layoffs, unfair promotions, bad company morale—any of these grievances can turn audiences hostile, even if those issues are unrelated to your topic.

Organizing the Persuasive Presentation

When selecting a method for organizing your persuasive presentation, it's critical to keep the audience attitudes in mind.

1) Proposition to Proof. In this method, you state your proposition right up front, at the beginning of your presentation. Then, prove your proposition using three to five points of evidence (Logos), emotional appeal (Pathos), and transitions to reinforce and connect your ideas.

Finally, review the evidence and end with a strong closing statement.

This method works well with favorable audiences, and is possible with some work for uninformed, apathetic and favorable mixed groups, but is not a good choice for a hostile or hostile-mix audience. They are likely to be immediately offended by whatever you present, and it will be difficult for you to overcome it. It is also effective when speaking to senior leaders. They want to know what you are proposing from the beginning, and rarely have the patience to sit through all types of explanation before getting to the point.

Example of a proposition to proof situation:

Proposition: "I recommend our corporation fund and operate an on-site day care facility."

Three Points of Proof:

•With their kids on-site, employees won't be stressed rushing to work on time or having to leave early to pick up children.

Transition: Not only will this reduce stress, but it will create happy, loyal staff who feel like their needs are being taken care of.

•Since on-site day care can be either fully or partially funded by the corporation, this provides a strong financial incentive for employees to stay with the corporation.

Transition: Another benefit of a day care is less absenteeism.

•Other corporations with on-site day care have reported only favorable results and cost savings due to less employee absenteeism.

Call to Action: "Let's meet next Thursday so we can make a decision. I urge all of you to see the benefits for both the company and its employees."

PERSUASIVE PLANNING WORKSHEET   PROPOSITION TO PROOF

Central Theme:

Consider: Purpose, Audience, and Logistics (PAL™)

Proposition:

Proof & Supporting Data:	Proof & Supporting Data:	Proof & Supporting Data:
	Transition →	Transition →

Introduction 10-15%

Grabber: Source Credibility:

W.I.I.F.T.?:   Preview (optional) :

Conclusion 5-10%

Review:

Memorable Statement/Appeal to Action:

© 2014/2015 (BRODY 215.886.1688 • BrodyPro.com

2) Motivated Sequence (Problem to Solution). This
method was developed by Alan Monroe at Purdue University
in the 1930s and is the method most used in sales. The
motivated sequence either identifies a need in audience
members, or makes them aware of a need. You really are
building a case that a problem exists. You then supply the
means to satisfy that need, or solve the problem.

Here are the five steps:
- **Attention:** Grab the audience's attention with a
  thought-provoking fact or statement.
- **Need:** Describe a need the audience members have or
  problem that needs to be solved. With logic and
  emotional appeals build their belief that
  something must be done.
- **Satisfaction:** Tell them how the need can be met, how
  their problem can be solved.
- **Visualization:** Describe the positive picture of what
  the future will look like with your proposed solution in
  place, and/or what it will be like without it.

- **Call to Action:** Tell the audience members what they need to do. Make your appeal for action.

Example of motivated sequence:

Attention: Are you holding yourself back in your career because of an inability to present and sell your ideas?

Need: In order to become an effective leader, you must be an effective presenter. Studies show ...

Satisfaction: If you take a BRODY workshop, you will learn to:
- Better organize your ideas
- Accurately read your audience
- Effectively control any stage fright
- Use effective visual aids
- Learn the art of persuasive presentations

Visualization: With these skills, you will be able to connect with your audience and sell your ideas. Picture yourself as a regional sales manager (head of your department, etc.) ...

Call to action: Telephone, fax, e-mail, or visit our Web site at: www.BrodyPro.com

Knowing how to present persuasively is critical to career development, and also will benefit you in other areas of your life. The ability to influence others' beliefs and motivate change is a powerful tool to be used carefully and selectively.

PERSUASIVE PLANNING WORKSHEET   MOTIVATED SEQUENCE

Central Theme:

Consider: Purpose, Audience, and Logistics (PAL™)

Problem or Need:

Solution or Satisfaction (features/benefits):

Visualization:

Transition →

Introduction   10-15%

Grabber:

Source Credibility:

W.I.I.F.T.?:

Preview (optional):

Conclusion   5-10%

Review/Q&A:

Appeal to Action:

© 2014/2015   BRODY   215.886.1688 • BrodyPro.com

3) Reflective. Using this method, the problem is stated and proven right in the beginning of the presentation. This works most effectively if the speaker and audience then agree on a criteria to evaluate each of the possible solutions and to ultimately make a decision.

After the problem and the criteria are agreed upon, solutions are offered and evaluated against the criteria. Effective speakers often present the positive points of each solution, then smash them with evidence to the contrary (using the agreed upon criteria as a basis of evaluation), and finally present the best solution—supporting it with plenty of evidence.

Warning: If you are not strong and compelling when presenting your beliefs, you will not be able to convince others that your way is the best. Leave no loopholes; make sure that you have eliminated other points of view as viable, leaving your solution as the best choice.

This is an excellent approach for analytical people who love to evaluate all possibilities. It can be overkill for favorable, uninformed, and apathetic audiences if they are not detail-oriented. This approach can work well with hostile and hostile-mixed groups.

Example of the reflective situation:

This starts the same way as the Motivated Sequence (Problem to Solution).

Problem: The turnover rate at our company among both men and women with young children is far above the national average. I am sure that you agree that we need to reverse this trend, if we are to keep our key employees and attract qualified candidates.

Agreement of Criteria: I think that to make a good decision, we need to consider cost, liability, and convenience. Do you agree? Are there others you think we should add? If not, let's look at possible solutions, weighing each against the criteria.

Solution #1: Do nothing.
Advantage:
  • Easiest thing to do

Disadvantages:
  • Won't solve the current problem
  • It won't help us attract new employees who have young children

Given the disadvantages, we can't afford to do nothing. Let's look at another solution.

Solution #2: Pay for off-site day care.
Advantage:
  • Liability criteria met

Disadvantages:
  • Cost prohibitive to most employees

- Totally inconvenient

Again, this won't work. Let's look at another possibility.

Solution #3: Build an on-site day care.

Disadvantage:
- Liability will be an issue

Advantages:
- Our attorney says we can overcome liability
- Convenience and economic benefit for employees

Call to action: I recommend, given the criteria, that we agree building an on-site day care facility to stop the turnover rate and help us attract quality workers is our best solution. Who will join me to set up a task force to move forward?

SPEECH PLANNING WORKSHEET		REFLECTIVE
Central Theme:		
Consider: Purpose, Audience, and Logistics (PAL™)		
Problem Definition:		
Criteria for Judging Possible Solutions:		
Possible Solution:	**Possible Solution:**	**Possible Solution:**
Positives:	**Positives:**	**Negatives:**
Negatives:	**Negatives:**	**Positives:**
Transition →	Transition →	
	Introduction 10-15%	
Grabber:	**Source Credibility:**	
W.I.I.F.T.?:	**Preview (optional):**	
	Conclusion 5-10%	
Review/Q&A:		
Memorable Statement/Appeal to Action:		

Of course, learning how to organize a persuasive speech will not be any use until you first learn the art of persuasion... and that's a great example of a transition to take you into the next chapter!

Key Takeaways
- Cluster your information in 3 to 5 main points
- Select a method of organization so the audience can follow
  - ✓ Informative
    - Chronological order
    - Spatial order
    - Topical order
    - Cause and effect
    - What? So what? Now what?
  - ✓ Persuasive
    - Proposition to proof
    - Motivated sequence (problem to solution)
    - Reflective
- Create an outline
- Write transitions to link ideas

Chapter 4

Use Stories & Examples to Create Unforgettable Impact

In Chapter 2, I talked about using examples and stories to help bring information to life, and to make the material "stick."

People love stories.

Did you know that we humans are actually "hard-wired" for stories? Long before we developed written language, our ancestors passed along their history and traditions orally. You could say it's in our genes to process information and make decisions based on stories.

They have an undeniable impact, opening minds and hearts and appealing to us on every level of our being. To immediately increase your relatability and engagement with your audience, include stories in your presentations.

Stories are Sticky

Stories have an interesting element to them. When people listen to your stories, they fill in the details and visuals with their imaginations, in effect co-creating them with you.

If, for example, you tell an anecdote about running down the platform to catch the last train before you'll be late for a meeting, your briefcase thudding against your leg as you run, listeners will picture the scene in their minds. If they've ever had a similar incident, they will relate strongly, but even if they haven't, picturing the scene causes them to make the story their own.

This leads to an effect known as "stickiness." Long after listeners have forgotten many of the details, statistics, or slides in your presentation, they'll remember your stories. The stories are what "sticks."

Take advantage of this stickiness by making sure you use stories, when possible, to illustrate your main points. You might have to do a fair amount of research and preparation to come up with the right stories, but it will definitely be worth it.

By the way, the best stories often don't come from books. They come from your own experiences.

Stories Generate a Near Experience

The most powerful way for someone to learn about something is to actually experience it. However, that isn't really possible in the confines of your presentation, is it? If you're attempting to persuade a group of the benefits of on-site day care, you're not about to take a field trip across town to another company's day care.

This is where stories come in.

Remember that old AT&T slogan? Even if you don't, it was: "AT&T is the next best thing to being there." A story is the next best thing to being there, because it gives your audience what's referred to as a "near experience."

Brain researchers have discovered that the parts of the brain associated with actually having an experience are engaged even when someone is *just hearing about an experience.* If you tell your audience members about the wind in your face as you missed the train and it flashed past you, the part of their brain that processes feeling on the skin activates. If you talk about the noise of the train thundering down the track, the part of their brain that processes hearing lights up. This is why reading fiction can be such a powerful experience you can hardly bear to put the book down.

Needless to say, the ability to give your audience these "near experiences" makes storytelling one of the most powerful speaking tools in your presentation arsenal. It enables you to transport your audience members to places they've never been.

Did you know that business storytelling can also enhance your leadership? We follow leaders because of their vision and the way they make us feel. Use stories to:

- **Communicate values:** Get across who you are and what's important to you as a person
- **Launch visions:** Use a story to get others excited about your vision
- **Teach lessons:** This is a classic use of storytelling throughout time, from the Brothers Grimm to the Bible
- **Humanize the leader:** show your human side to your audience, allowing them to bond, empathize, and connect with you and your message

Give Your Story Engaging Content

Don't just recite something dry like a police or newspaper report—this is not a story. Remember that famous line in the old Dragnet TV show? "Just the facts ma'am."

That's the opposite of how to tell an engaging story. Yes, you do need to include the facts, but add some flavor and color with:

- Scene Development: Give a few details so listeners can picture the setting and what's happening. "The wind was whipping the rain into my face."
- Character Development: Add details to help listeners picture the characters; bring them to life. "He was one of those guys you wouldn't want to run into in a dark alley."
- Action: Use active words, show the characters in action. Don't just say, "I missed the train." Say, "I slammed (action word!) right up against the door as it closed, and had to yank my briefcase out before the train took off with it stuck in the door."
- Character Emotion: What kind of emotions did the characters exhibit?
- Dialogue: Help listeners hear the exchange between the characters. "So I said, ..."

Give the Story Some Heart – Yours!

Your body language and voice are going to have a direct impact on the listeners' experience and how much your story comes alive for them. Get into it by:

- being vocally animated
- acting out elements of the story with gestures and facial expressions (don't go overboard, practice in the mirror to make sure you don't become clownish)
- changing your voice slightly as you play different roles (e.g. lowering your voice when you give the dialogue your dad said to you as a kid)
- being sensitive to timing; don't rush through it; pause for strategic effect

Find the Appropriate Balance

I'm not trying to talk you into becoming a Broadway performer. A professional presentation will not have the same feel to it as sitting around a campfire spinning tales, nor should it. You're a presenter — quite possibly in a serious area of endeavor with high expectations of professionalism. Always use stories, but at the same time, always use discretion, remember your subject matter, your goal, and your audience.

When should you use a story in your presentation?

To illustrate a major point. Stories grab and hold attention, so they are the perfect tool to drive home a point in a way your audience will easily integrate, and even better, remember. If the point or topic is somewhat controversial, a story might be the perfect way of changing people's perceptions in a gentle yet powerful way.

To break up otherwise dry information. It's even harder to hold people's attention if your material is dry, factual, statistical, or theoretical. But dry, factual information or theories can -- and should -- be brought to life with examples, anecdotes and stories. In this way, you are sharing the necessary content in an engaging, attention-keeping manner. It's worth the effort to go out of your way in the preparation phase of your presentation to come up with stories that will liven up your content.

Give your audience members a laugh, a tear, a gasp, and you'll keep them hungry for more.

Stories don't have to be dramatic. Look for these gems everywhere in your life, stories others can relate to, stories that show you as humble or human, stories that shaped your thinking or taught you something. Practice telling them in an engaging fashion, practice tying in your points, practice your delivery in the mirror and in front of other people ... practice, practice, practice.

Story Checklist

Frequently, stories are the only things people remember from a presentation, so telling them well is important. Once you've decided on which stories to include, you'll want to practice your delivery. Telling a story should sound natural, like you're talking to a friend. I'm including this storytelling checklist to help you make sure your stories will be memorable.

I suggest taping your story, and listening to the playback when you fill out this checklist.

<u>Structure</u>

- ❏ **Logical Flow / Easy to Follow**

- ❏ **Adequate Set-up to Understand the Context**

- ❏ **Rising Action Building Toward a Climax**

- ❏ **Ending That Helped Make the Point of Story Clear (Resolution)**

- ❏ **Appropriate Length**

Content

- ❏ **Scene Development (you could picture the scene)**

- ❏ **Character Development (you could picture the characters)**

- ❏ **Action**

- ❏ **Character Emotion (emotion accompanied the action)**

- ❏ **Dialogue (you could "hear" the characters and their exchanges)**

Delivery

- ❏ **Delivered with Feeling**

- ❏ **Body Language**

- ❏ **Role Playing**

- ❏ **Vocal Animation**

- ❏ **Timing/Pauses**

Key Takeaways

- People love stories
- Stories are effective because they help people think/feel/act
- Look to your own life examples to share

Chapter 5

Visual Aids in Focus

"Knowledge is a process of piling up facts; wisdom lies in their simplification." ~ Martin H. Fischer, physicist and author

OK. You are probably thinking, "You haven't even mentioned PowerPoint yet." Your wait is over! Now's the time.

Keep in mind that slideware is meant to reinforce your information, not **be** the information.

Now that you know what you are talking about – including the "storyline" and key points – you can step back and determine where (or if) you want to use slides.

Why are visual aids, like slide shows, important to a presentation?

Many people have to see it to believe it, and sometimes just to understand it.

Approximately 65% of all people are visual learners, and studies have shown that our ability to retain information increases by almost 40 percent when visual aids are used.

So, don't just *tell* your audience about a process; diagram it, chart it, graph it, photograph it … illustrate it visually in the most clear and direct way you can imagine.

Although speakers can, and should, create pictures with words, actual visuals remain an important presentation component. Used wisely, they enhance communication in a way that nothing else can.

> **Presentation Tip:** Be so well prepared that you can still speak if the electricity goes out or the equipment fails. The best visual is a really good speaker. You may well decide visual aids are not even necessary.

We've all heard the term "death by PowerPoint." Use of this and other presentation tools can be easily *misused or overused.*

Don't get so comfortable using one type of visual aid, such as PowerPoint, that you won't try anything else. After all, terrific new technologies come along all the time. There are many kinds of visual aids available; a presentation you've given 50 times takes on new life by changing the type of visual aids.

Slides are for the audience members' benefit — not yours!

- Do you create your slide decks so you won't forget what comes next?
- Do you create slide decks to do the "heavy lifting," so you don't have to explain it all?
- Do you create slide decks to serve as handouts?

The real purpose of slide decks is to help the live audience more fully understand and remember the presentation content. Take your presentations to the next level by making your audience your first priority.

> **Presentation Tip:** You can always create a second, more detailed, slide deck to be used as a handout or takeaway.

KSDS (Keep Slide Decks Simple!)

That phrase should be your motto. When creating a slide deck for presentation, keep these guidelines in mind:

- short phrases, not sentences or paragraphs – better yet, use pictures

- legible sans-serif fonts—18 points or bigger

This is 18 point size.
This is 22 point size.
This is 24 point size.

- no more than two font styles
- upper/lower case (never ALL CAPS, they're hard to read)
- 2 to 5 high-contrast colors
- simple backgrounds
- one message per chart
- descriptive title
- minimal clutter
- contrasting colors with plain backgrounds
- no keys, codes, or vertical labels
- animated builds for lists
- highlight key numbers

Look for every opportunity to use pictures and graphics. After all, we're talking about a visual medium. Projecting words is not visual!

Be careful not to do a "data dump" on your slides.

Here are three "before and after" examples.

Before | ## After

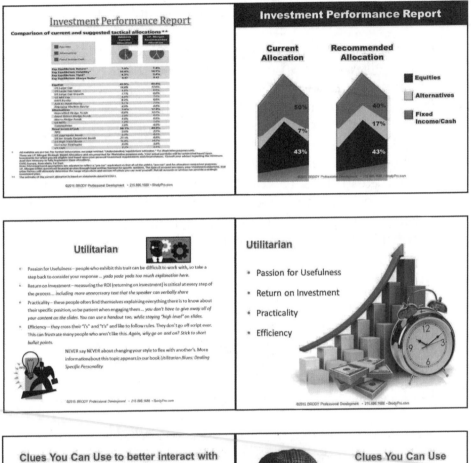

Graphs & charts enhance visual aids.

These images help an audience grasp your point, make comparisons, or view specific items in relation to the whole. Some examples include...

- *Profile graphs* use shading underneath the data, and make it easy to see large or significant changes.

- *Bar graphs* let your audience see blocks of information, allowing them to quickly make visual comparisons. Use a bar graph (or column chart) when you want your audience to focus on the actual figures, not any trends – these best illustrate relative quantities.

- *Line graphs* (aka "fever charts") make it easy to illustrate trends, to compare over a long time, and show increases or decreases in a quick way. They are usually best to illustrate a growth point or movement, not an actual analysis of the

 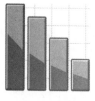

Profile Graph   **Bar Graph**   **Line Graph**

- *Pie charts* clearly depict pieces (or "wedges") in relation to the whole ("pie") and to one another. Do not create more than seven sections as it will be difficult to understand.

- *Organizational charts* help to clarify complex subjects or procedures. They are useful to detail social groups/relationships, or chains of command. They can help your audience quickly see and understand your subject.

- *Flowcharts* show a series of sequences or relationships in an easy-to-follow format. They are effective for illustrating a process through steps or stages.

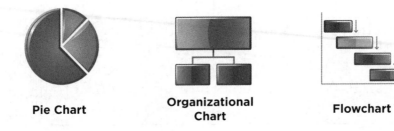

Pie Chart   **Organizational Chart**   **Flowchart**

Chart design tips:

- Make headings active, not passive (i.e. "Results of Incentive Contests" is better than "2009-2014 Sales").
- Use bold colors like dark blue, purple, orange, red, black and green. Ensure there is contrast between the various colors. Also, avoid using red and green together since colorblind people have difficulty differentiating them.
- Use big, bold fonts so the entire audience can read the visual aid.
- Keep your chart easy to read, not packed with data. The viewer only has a few seconds to grasp your point.

Using Power Point? Take advantage of these features:

- **The Presenter View Option:** Enables you to see future slides, while only showing the audience the current one. Invaluable for making sure you can transition effectively without having to memorize the deck. Also shows a clock and a view of your notes.

- **The No-Slide Element:** Blanking out your screen makes it possible to capture the full, undivided attention of the audience. Press the "B" key on your keyboard or use a remote with a blanking option.

- **Move Directly to Any Slide:** Type its number and press the Enter key (i.e. "8" then enter or "15" and then enter). Have a numbered list of your slides sitting next to your laptop for reference, and you'll be able to move all over your deck with ease. (Particularly helpful for the Q & A, when you want to reference different slides to give an answer.)

> **Presentation Tip:** Set your computer so that no screen saver or power savers come on. Sometimes two computers are attached to the same projector; make sure you know how to switch between the two when it's your turn to present.

Jazz up your presentations with tips and products from these innovative sites:

www.microsoft.com/office/powerpoint (great site to visit for how-to articles and tech support)

www.digitaljuice.com (purchase a great product called Digital Juice for PowerPoint)

www.dailywav.com (find interesting sounds and voices for more relaxed special occasion presentations)

Handouts — Still Useful After All These Years

Make sure your handouts provide genuine value, and are not just a printout of a slide with one photo or line of text on it! Those will wind up in the trash. Handouts can be used when your presentation contains too much technical information to include, when you don't want your audience to take notes, as a pre-read, or when you want to offer added value.

If people want the slides to reference following the presentation, and you want to be "green," you can also give the audience members a thumb drive containing your handouts, or a link where they can download them from your Web site.

Handout Dos:

- Do give out copies of charts, slides, graphs or other visual aids.
- Do provide an outline of your key points, including relevant information you have chosen not to mention in your presentation.
- Do make sure handouts are neat, proofread, and contain your name, address, and telephone number (if you would like your audience members to contact you).
- Do, if appropriate, include biographical information about yourself, and some background facts about your company or service.

Presentation Tip: Tell audience members what information is available in the handout, so they can decide when, or if, to take notes. If you don't want them reading the handouts during your presentation, give them out at the end.

Remember -- a good visual aid does not make up for a poorly prepared or delivered presentation. Don't depend on your visuals to carry you – instead, you should think of them as a reinforcement tool.

Always be prepared to speak without them ... just in case!

Room Arrangements

Of course, it doesn't matter that you have great visuals if the audience can't see them. In Chapter 1, we discussed the "L" in PAL™ – Logistics. One logistic is the room arrangement. I know that you can't always get the room you'd like, but you can always ask. Pictured on the next page are some of the standard room arrangements that speakers can choose from, depending on the audience size.

Keep in mind when participants can see each other as well as the speaker and his/her visuals, it will create more energy in the room.

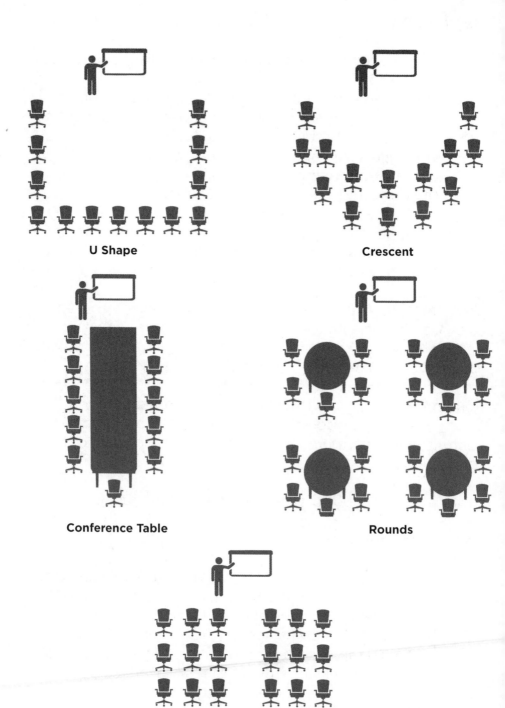

U Shape

Crescent

Conference Table

Rounds

Theater Style

Chapter 6

Putting It All Together: A Presentation in Three Acts

You've already done the heavy lifting – brainstormed and researched ideas, looked for supporting materials that anchored the facts and figures, determined what method of organization you wanted to use, created visuals, and then organized the information into three to five key ideas.

So, what's missing? An introduction and conclusion! Not to mention a need to edit what you have already put together. So, how do you put together the whole presentation? You do it by organizing your presentation into three separate parts:

- Grab their attention and set expectations with your **introduction.**
- Make your points and sway their opinion with the **body.**
- Sum it all up and leave them with your main point ringing in their ears with the **conclusion.**

The Introduction

"There are no second chances to make a first impression."
– attributed to many people, and paraphrased in many ways.

The introduction is how you start delivering a presentation – but remember, you've already written the body. It's hard – and a waste of time – to write the introduction first, because you don't exactly know what you are introducing.

Once you've written the body, then go back and ask yourself the following questions:
- How do I capture their attention?
- What is in it for them (after all, they will be asking themselves this question)?
- What do they need to know about me to ensure credibility?
- What type of overview do I want to give them?

- When will I take their questions?

Your introduction is the time and place to tell the audience members what you are going to be talking to them about. Your introduction should take up approximately 10 percent of your presentation. Don't rush it.

Regardless of the type of presentation you're giving, avoid this clichéd and boring opening: "Good morning, my name is _____, and I am so glad to be here talking to you today about _____."

Audience members already know your name ... or they don't care. They also couldn't care less that you're happy to be here ... they're here for themselves, not you!

Use the opening to grab their attention, break their preoccupation – whether with their cell phones or thinking about all of the things they need to do -- and get them intrigued, excited, or at least interested. They will be interested because you're making it clear just how your presentation hits their needs. Create that rapport before giving them the main content.

Remember, your introduction serves four purposes:

1. Get the audience's attention
2. Establish WIIFT? (What's In It For Them)
3. Establish your credibility and create rapport
4. Let the audience members know where you are going with the presentation and when they can ask questions

Grab the audience's attention (and don't let go).

You must get your audience's attention right away. If you start out slowly, you may never get audience members' attention. Focus their attention on you from the get-go using a **grabber statement** or **hook** to reel them in.

This can take many forms. You can tell a story, give an example, ask a rhetorical question, make a controversial statement, use a quote, or use humor. Here are some examples of grabbers that will surely get an audience's attention.

- **Ask a question (real or rhetorical):** Did you know our industry was labeled "recession proof" by CNBC just last week?

By asking a question, you give your audience something to think about or react to.

In this case, audience members may be thinking, "Then why is there a hiring freeze and a wage freeze? What's going on here?"

- **State an unusual fact:** Walmart averages a profit of $1.8 million every hour.

- **Give an illustration, example or story:** Paint a mental picture for your audience members by telling them a story that relates to your subject. This will get their attention and make the content real for them.

  For example, "When I took over running this company, my grandfather took me out to lunch, ordered two dry-aged steaks and a bottle of expensive champagne. He proceeded to bend my ear for an hour, giving me all sorts of old-school business advice. I didn't get one word in. One of the things he warned me about was trying to take the company too big too fast, but I didn't listen, because by the time he got to that particular point – I had had a bit too much of the bubbly. Isn't it great that I didn't listen?"

- **Use a quotation:** Catchy phrases and quotes are great openers as long as they're not overused to the point of cliché. Look online for unusual quotes, or quotes from unusual people. Here's one from Steve

Jobs: "Quality is much better than quantity. One home run is much better than two doubles."

- **Use humor:** Again, humor can be tricky. Make sure it's in good taste, and relevant to your speech. Always use your best judgment. Humor at someone's expense is never funny. Humor at your own expense can be funny, as long as it's not overly self-deprecating. When in doubt, leave it out.

WIIFT? (What's In It For Them?): This is so important, I'll repeat it numerous times throughout the book. Don't wait too long to get to this point, or you'll lose your audience's attention very quickly. This is particularly true for any audience whose attendance is mandatory. Bottom line: Why should they care about the topic?

Pique their interest quickly with an attention grabber. Then immediately make the connection between that attention grabber and something important to your listeners. What are their issues? What are they struggling with? What do they need right now? What might incentivize them to take the actions you'll be suggesting or agree with your proposals?

No matter how dedicated to a company or career, people tend to put themselves first. Take advantage of this normal facet of human nature by determining what could make someone care about your proposal or presentation, and make sure those elements are in the opening of your talk. It's not enough just to grab their attention – you have to hold it. You do that by appealing to your audience's self-interest.

If you are facing hostile or captive audience members, what might you possibly present that could be a benefit to them? If you consider these questions when preparing your presentation, you will grab their attention and hold it while they wait to hear more.

Is what you are proposing going to be lucrative for the company, and also for them? Explain how. Will it open new opportunities for them? Get those ideas in up front. Will it solve an existing problem and make their lives better or easier in any way? Tell them! Be selective with your information. You don't need to tell an audience everything at the outset.

By presenting your information with WIIFT? in mind, you'll know how to influence your audience.

Let them know who you are: If everyone in the room already knows who you are, skip this step. If not, establish your credentials and credibility early on. If you're being introduced by someone who listed your credentials—please don't repeat them. In fact, whether or not there will be someone introducing you is something you should know in advance, so you can prepare the appropriate introduction to deliver for them.

Although I've been introduced many times, I always try to add something at the beginning of my presentation that wasn't part of the planned introduction. Sometimes I refer to something that might have just happened at the conference. If you are speaking at a big conference or meeting and you will be introduced, prepare your own introduction and send it to the person who will be introducing you.

Bring an extra copy to the event. Ask the person to read what you wrote -- that way you get the setup you want, one that flows seamlessly into the intro of your talk.

Preview your subject: Although your audience probably knows the purpose of your presentation, and a general idea of the subject matter, it helps them to hear from you what you'll be talking about.

If you're giving an informative presentation, tell the audience what you will be covering.

If your goal is to persuade, you don't have to be quite so specific. For example, don't say, "I'm here to convince you ..."

That will immediately put people on the defensive.

It's always a good idea for you to tell the audience members when you will take questions. The perfect time to tell them is in this preview. More on the topic of the Q&A is in chapter 19.

The Body

Spend about 80 to 85 percent of your time on the body of your presentation.

By now you will already have written or outlined the body of your presentation.

Remember ...
- Divide your material into three to five main points.
- Then, support each point with the data (but not just facts and figures).
- Connect the main points with transitions.
- When planning your presentation, think of it as an accordion – it can expand or contract depending on timing.

As a reminder, once you have written the body, check to see that you have included some of the following to enhance your facts and figures:

- Examples – add interest
- Stories
- Quotations – must be a well-known and reputable source to have value
- Definitions – can help you prove a point or make a point easier to understand
- Comparisons – present similarities
- Contrasts – present differences
- Statistics – numerical facts and figures supporting your points
- Analogies
- Metaphors
- Humor

- Audience involvement
- Visual aids
- Emotional appeals

Using Transitions

To achieve continuity throughout your presentation, use the transitional phrases we discussed earlier. Transitional phrases should be fully written out and easy to read.

Use them:

- To move you from the introduction to the body of your presentation
- As you move from point to point within the presentation
- To move from the body to the conclusion.

Helpful transitional phrases:

"Now that we've looked at ... let's move on to ..."
"We've established the criteria for ... we can now look at ..."
"And this leads me to a completely different point..."

The Conclusion

People tend to remember what they hear first and what they hear last. This is called "primacy recency." Although the conclusion is short (5% of your time), it is critical. Don't rush it -- because your closing remarks are the last thing your audience will hear, and probably remember. They should neatly reinforce and tie together everything that came before. Inexperienced or nervous presenters often miss this important final opportunity.

Be sure to:

- Review and emphasize your main points -- briefly!

- Include a strong call to action if you want audience members to do something in particular, like move forward with a particular project, find a team, hire new people, etc.

- Provide closure to your presentation by giving the audience something to remember.

The famous conclusion to John F. Kennedy's 1961 inaugural address is a fantastic example of a memorable close: "Ask not what your country can do for you, ask what you can do for your country." Short, to the point and unforgettable.

How can you come up with such an impressive close?

Follow the same examples used in the opening: ask a question; state an unusual fact; give an illustration, example or story; or present a quotation. Or, challenge the audience members to take a specific action.

If you use your opening grabber, add a new ending or insight. For example: "If you want your streets and your children to be safer, consider what was presented here tonight, and vote, 'Yes' on the new skateboard park."

This is called "book ending" – when you start and end using the same point. If your goal is to get commitment and action, you need to ask for it – don't assume the audience will put all of the pieces together.

Guidelines for Effective Conclusions

- Draw conclusions for the audience
- Suggest action or next steps
- Ask for a commitment
- Keep it to 5 percent or less of your presentation
- Write it out and really practice it
- End your conclusion on a positive note
- Test your conclusion with these questions:
  - ✓ Does it bring closure to the presentation?
  - ✓ Did I get the results I wanted?

If the answers to these questions are both "yes," you've come to a successful conclusion.

> **Presentation Tip:** Divide your conclusion into three parts – first it is a review, then open for questions, and finally, close with your memorable statement.

It's Time to Edit

Now it's time to start editing – really editing. Most presentations suffer from "infobesity." Think about how long it took you to know the material (two months? two years?). Why do you think the audience will "get it" in 20 minutes? Go back and analyze your presentation. Determine what you must cover, and what can be cut. Once you've done that, go back again and determine the "must know," the "should know" and the "could know."

Must Know, Should Know, Could Know:

This can be done in two ways:

- Have your 3 to 5 main points with must, should and could know information under each point.

- Or, you can have point #1, must know, point #2, should know, etc.

Most presentations run longer than speakers anticipate, often due to technical difficulties, interruptions and questions, or starting late. By organizing your information into these three categories, you'll know what to eliminate if you run out of time.

> **Presentation Tip:** If you're running out of time, please do not compensate by speaking faster to get all the information in. It will make you sound nervous, it will make your audience nervous, and they'll leave with their heads spinning, without absorbing any of the information you were so desperate to impart.

Plan ahead, so you're prepared and unflustered if you do have to shorten your presentation.

Writing Your Final Draft

I recommend the following old school approach:

1. Use 8 1/2 x 11 inch paper – stiff stock – not index cards, as they tend to get mixed up and are hard to read.

2. Write on only the top two-thirds of the page, so you don't move your eyes down or drop your chin, which makes your voice drop as well.

3. To make the final draft readable, use at least 18-point font size, bold letters. Or, if you are hand writing it, use a medium point felt-tip pen rather than a ballpoint pen.

4. Decide where to use visual aids; make notes in the margins of your draft, and number each visual.

5. Use short phrases with enough information to keep your presentation on track but not so much that you read them verbatim. Do write out your opening grabber, your transitions and any facts or figures you must include, along with the final close. Don't just write single words; you may forget what you want to say.

6. Color-code your presentation: must know, should know, could know. That way, you know what to cut if timing is a problem.

If you don't want hard copy notes, you can use speakers' notes on PowerPoint slides – just be sure to make the font big enough. Limit what you write and be sure to include transitions from slide to slide.

I always get the question of whether I need to use notes. You don't have to have notes, but they provide a good safety net. My goal is to be able to glance at them – easily – but not depend on them.

Chapter 7
The Art of Persuasion

Have you ever ordered anything while watching HSN, QVC, or an infomercial? These presenters brilliantly make a case for things you neither want nor need, and they do it so well that the temptation to buy is high.

Have you ever bought a magazine subscription from someone who came to your door? These appeals can be equally effective.

Infomercials and well-trained sales pitches are both examples of the power of the persuasive presentation. In chapters 1-3, I talked about the purpose of a presentation (inform, persuade and entertain), knowing your audience (favorable, uninformed, apathetic, hostile and mixed), and how to organize your presentation – particularly for persuasion (proposition to proof, motivated sequence and reflective).

Aristotle said that all speaking is persuasive speaking (you are always selling yourself and your ideas) – and I agree – however, it's worth delving a little deeper when it comes to persuasion.

How can you be persuasive in your presentations?

Aristotle talked about three methods of persuasion: Logos, Pathos, and Ethos. These concepts are just as valid today as they were in his time, over two thousand years ago.

Logos is the Greek word for reason, and is the root of the word logic.

Of course you start by organizing your presentation in a logical manner, making it easy for the listeners to follow. Then, you include logos by introducing facts and figures, statistics, studies, and other forms of documentation.

This information can be slanted, by only including the information that supports your premise. Politicians offer the clearest example of this tactic.

Speaking on the exact same issue, one politician will try to convince you that raising taxes is the only way to improve things. His or her opponent will try to persuade you that lowering taxes is the only way. They will each provide the pertinent facts, statistics, and studies that "prove" their argument—and leave out those which do not.

Unbalanced? Sure.

Persuasive? You bet!

Presentation Tip: Of course, whose "logic" are we using? Be aware that your perspective is most likely slanted and you will use sources that support your point of view.

Usually, people will go for the lower tax idea up front, but a particularly persuasive politician can convince voters that increasing taxes is a good thing. You might need this level of persuasive ability, if what you are proposing is likely to be unpopular with your audience.

Logos also requires a logical progression of ideas, so lay out your information in a way that will make sense to your audience and lead them to the conclusion you want them to reach. Logic appeals to the mind, but there is much more to persuasion than that.

Pathos, also from the Greek, refers to using emotions. It appeals to the heart, and to the needs, wants, and desires of your audience members. Most human decisions are made using a combination of logic and emotion (logos and pathos).

To persuade, you'll need both, along with a solid understanding of your audience's needs. If you lay out a strong, logical argument, but fail to take into account how your audience members feel about something (emotion), you will not succeed. On the other hand, an appeal directed solely at their hearts will not have a lasting impact. The power of it will fade over time, as do most emotions.

That's why sharing heartwarming stories and examples resonate. For example, sharing a picture of a starving child gets more donations than seeing the statistics. People make decisions emotionally and justify logically.

Think about it. If highly charged topics like gun control, same-sex marriage and capital punishment could be presented by using logic, there would be less disagreement.

Ethos is all about your credibility – real and perceived. How are you perceived by your audience? Factors include your...
- education
- degrees
- age
- gender
- reputation
- title/position in your company
- presence

Of course, with the increased prevalence of soical media, your number of Facebook friends, Twitter followers, or even your Klout score might also influence your credibility!

Three Components of Credibility

Credibility is all about the audience's perception of you:
- perceived trustworthiness
- perceived competence
- perceived conviction

Credibility is vital, because when people trust you, they're more willing to listen, to believe what you're saying, and take the course of action you're recommending. And that's persuasion, isn't it?

Tips to establish credibility:

- Establish competence. Be sure the audience members are aware of your credentials and accomplishments. Be careful that you don't come across as a braggart.
- Establish convictions as you demonstrate your knowledge and speak with authority, passion, and of course, conviction. Your delivery comes into play here!
- Trustworthiness is a bit trickier to establish. A classic approach is to establish common ground, sharing similarities between you and your audience.

For example: "I've lived in Cheltenham for the past 25 years and I'm a product of their public schools, just like many of you. I've also been paying the township's high taxes for the past 25 years, like many of you. And like you, I want to pay less."

You've now established common ground and a common goal – your mutual dissatisfaction with the taxes you pay. All these common bonds count toward establishing trust, but nothing unites people faster than a common goal.

Successful presentations usually combine logos, pathos, and ethos. Your topic, your own presentation style, and the makeup and needs of your audience will help you determine how much of each to use.

Persuasion Secrets from Great Salespeople

Even if you aren't a "salesperson" per se, you *are* selling your own credibility along with your ideas!

1) Features Tell; Benefits Sell

When persuading others to agree, to act, to release funds, to purchase, to sign a contract, to volunteer, to *anything* ... don't just describe the attributes of your plan. Don't tell them about it, tell them why they want it and need it. Always give your audience the benefits they will receive. Don't assume they will understand them without you pointing them out, and don't ever assume they don't care about the benefits.

> **Presentation Tip:** If you're pitching an idea or service/product, **benefit is king.**

For example, think of the introduction of the *time-released capsule* (feature) into a market already filled with cold remedies. "Feel better *all day long* with one pill (benefit)!"

How about introducing an innovative new mattress into a market filled with down, memory-foam, pillow-top, and adjustable beds? How would you sell it, first in development to your own company, then to mattress stores, and ultimately the weary, sleep-deprived consumer? If you were as savvy as the folks at the Sleep Number Bed, you'd have your benefits front and center: DualAir Technology allows each person to adjust *their side of the bed* (benefit) to their own hardness or softness comfort level! Finally, a decent night's sleep in bed *with your partner* (benefit).

If you're trying to get funding for a new company initiative, don't just list the benefits to the company — make sure to create a bridge showing how higher company profits will directly affect your audience as well. (Bigger team budgets, satisfaction of being a part of something ground-breaking, jobs saved and added, opportunities for promotion, etc.)

Remember, WIIFM? (What's in it for me?) is human nature. Probably always will be. Take advantage of this immutable fact and tell your audience *exactly what's in it for them!* Make it easy for them to do what you are recommending. Are you presenting the benefits clearly and powerfully enough to persuade?

Try this exercise: Have someone ask you "So what?" each time you state a feature, give a statistic, or offer a suggestion or idea without including a benefit. You want to get so that answering the "So what?" question is second nature. This is the benefit.

2) Objections are Your Friends

In the world of persuasive speaking, nothing is more frustrating than audience members who will not say "yes," but won't tell you why. You don't know how to respond, because you don't know what's standing in the way of agreement. If they would just object to something, you could fashion an effective response.

If you stay open, non-defensive, and really listen, objections can offer invaluable information, by exposing exactly what is standing in the way of audience members buying into your proposition. Remember, do this in advance of your presentation if possible.

3) Close the Deal

Please, don't go through all the trouble of making a brilliant and compelling case and then just wait to see if your audience responds. Even at the risk of rejection, be courageous and ask for a decision. Ask for agreement. Ask for the funding. Ask for what you need.

Don't be passive, or your audience might be the same. Lead the way with a strong call to action.

Remember, the art of persuasion is not some mysterious attribute some have and some don't. It's based on specific principles anyone can master, with understanding and practice.

Key Pointers

- To be persuasive, you need to use:
  - ✓ Logos (logic)
  - ✓ Pathos (emotion)
  - ✓ Ethos (credibility)
- People buy benefits, they don't buy features.
- Don't be afraid of objections.
- Ask for what you want

Chapter 8

Facilitative Presentations Engage Audiences

Spare them the monologue ... and start a dialogue

Modern audiences want to be part of the discussion.
In other words, they are looking for an exchange — a
two-way street. Smart presenters recognize this and
take advantage of it by actively encouraging audience
participation. Presenting in a facilitative style is all about
promoting a discussion.

This has many advantages over the traditional style of
presenting, where one person offers information, and others
listen, forming opinions they never get to share. It can also
be daunting to the presenter, who needs to get across his or
her information in the allotted time, and keep control of the
entire presentation.

Audience participation can be more time consuming than
expected; it can veer in unwanted directions, or even turn
hostile.

When considering the facilitative style, presenters wonder,
"How can I cover everything I need to cover if people in the
audience are using up valuable time with their comments?"

Resolve this quandary by making room for audience
participation during the presentation planning stage. If
you've been given 30 minutes to present, don't give yourself
30 (or 40!) minutes of material to cover. If you're truly
committed to facilitating audience participation, you need to
have only 15 minutes' worth of material.

But why should you be fully committed to audience participation?
- It can provide a much richer audience experience
- It can allow you to source ideas, questions and
  information from your audience

- It can leave people feeling included, inspired, and more willing to agree with your propositions and plans. Two basic human needs are to feel included, and to feel listened to. Facilitative presenting allows you to fulfill these needs in your audiences.

Be deliberate when planning for audience participation in your presentations:

- Identify specifically where in your presentation it would be good to invite participation, and indicate that in your outline.
- Work out how you're going to invite participation. What are you going to say? Write this down as well. Carefully craft the wording of your discussion questions, ahead of time.
- Set the tone with the wording of your questions, and explain what you hope the results of the discussion will be. For instance, "I'd like to hear what you have to say on this specific issue, to see if we can come to an agreement on our next steps moving forward."
- Plan how you want to use the discussion to move your message along. How will you transition out of the discussion into your next point?
- Allocate more time for the participation. A general rule of thumb is to prepare, plan and practice to go 50% of the allocated time when there is occasional interaction, questions and facilitation. For a highly interactive and facilitated presentation, you may only have 25% of the time dedicated to "content."

Logistics factor into facilitative presenting as well. Audiences seated lecture style are less likely to participate than those seated in a way that allows them to see each other. It's much better, when possible, that the room is arranged in a U shape, at a conference table, or in rounds. This was covered in Chapter 5.

Facilitative Presentation Tip: Summarize what people say after they've made their comments.

For example, you might have someone who talks about the importance of making sure that a particular project has the necessary funding. Before calling on someone else, you can summarize with: "I hear what you're saying. We need adequate funding for multiple reasons, including deadline pressures."

Repeating and summarizing keeps those who couldn't hear the speaker in the loop, and provides an excellent way to transition to another contributor.

Sometimes it helps to take a page from the world of training and write comments on a flip chart or white board. This encourages participation by showing you value what's being said enough to write it down. It also provides a menu of ideas to go back to, as you encourage more discussion.

The trickiest part of facilitative presenting is definitely controlling the discussion and time. By this, I don't mean censoring people's opinions. I mean making sure their comments stay on topic, and no one person dominates the room. If one person is allowed to do all the talking, the other members of your audience will shut down in annoyance, and they will not participate.

Strategies for keeping things under control:

- Politely interrupt a dominant talker, summarize what he or she has said, and immediately ask, *by name*, for a comment from someone else.
- During the presentation, reference the clock and the need for some audience members to get out on time.
- Learn to refocus the discussion if it wanders off topic or heads in a direction you don't want it to go. For instance, "Let's get back to our main topic." Use your presentation's main theme as your home base, to keep the discussion grounded.
- Ask questions of specific people in your audience, those you know have something favorable to offer.
- If you know in advance that a dominant person will be

in your audience, sit down with this person and ask for input on your presentation planning. He or she will gain a sense of ownership and, consequently, say less.

Doing a straight lecture is a lot easier and more efficient than inviting audience participation; but, the extra engagement of a facilitated discussion creates a stronger experience for everyone — including you. After you've done a few of them, you might never want to give a straight talk again.

Key points to remember:

- Audiences want to be included; look for ways and times to do so.
- Allow time for audience participation.
- Practice techniques to keep control.

Chapter 9
Speaking to Senior Management

"When written in Chinese, the word 'crisis' is composed of two characters. One represents danger and the other represents opportunity." ~John F. Kennedy

Any opportunity to present to senior management, or any decision makers in your company, can be a career maker — or breaker.

You are speaking to powerful people who hold your career in their hands; that's stressful in and of itself. Senior management may also frequently interrupt, take control of the presentation away from you, and throw you off your game.

There are some unique challenges and pitfalls to these situations. Let's explore these challenges.

The first one is perspective — yours versus theirs. It may be different in ways you never considered.

When you prepare to present before senior management, you'll probably be thinking as a manager. In contrast, the people you'll be speaking to will most likely be listening from their perspective as leaders.

There's an important difference between the two that you need to understand. Take a look at this chart from *Harvard Business Review's* John Kotter.

Manager
Plans
Produces Consistency
Produces Orderly Results

Leader
Sets Direction
Produces Movement
Produces Change

We could explain these lists by saying managers are tactics-oriented, while senior leaders are more strategy- and "big-picture"-oriented.

Therefore, when you present to a leadership audience, you need to integrate the strategic, big picture considerations into your material. Make it more about the direction that is being proposed or taken, and less about the nuts and bolts, day-to-day procedures of how to navigate that direction.

Presentation Tip: Remember, senior leadership produces movement and change. Mirror this in your presentation: Show your willingness to manage change and emphasize movement toward better results.

Get to the Point

Have you ever given a presentation to senior management, only to find them impatient, distracted, or continually interrupting to ask for information they would hear shortly, if they'd only let you speak?

You might be surprised how many presentations senior managers have to sit through. Imagine having a full plate of responsibilities while your day is eaten away by meetings and presentations.

Keep that in mind when you prepare and practice your presentation. Avoid data dumping or detailing every step of complex plans or systems ... and give them exactly what they need to know, as clearly and concisely as possible. This is not the time for show-boating, bonding, or humorous anecdotes about your kids.

Consider these two approaches:

- State your conclusion first, right at the beginning of your presentation. Then provide a lean, tight explanation of the "why" behind your conclusion.
- Work toward your conclusion, but work toward it quickly so that your audience is swept along in your momentum.

Prepare for Maximum Flexibility

It's not uncommon for senior managers to request a presenter's slides in advance of the presentation. The benefit? It enables them to get up to speed on the topic and engage the presenter faster.

The downside for you, the presenter? It's the same thing, their ability to engage faster.

Let me explain. Have you ever been three slides into your presentation only to be ordered to a later slide that a senior executive became concerned about when previewing the deck? You're in no position to say, "I'll get to that in a few minutes." No, you have to go right to it and, in the process, disrupt the planned flow of your message.

In preparation for this likely scenario:
- Gather any back-up information you may need and plan fast access. Create a slide appendix with this information.
- Anticipate "side roads" and plot the way back. "If this comes up, how will I tie it back to my main point?"
- Print out a slide list and be ready to jump.
- *Remember ...* Your objective is not to get through all the material.

> **Presentation Tip:** Create two slide decks. Senior management meetings often contain multiple presentations, meaning later presenters can easily wind up with their allotted times cut because previous presenters ran over. This could lead to a hurried presentation that reflects poorly on you — if you are one of the presenters whose time was shortened.

Beat a potential time crunch by creating an "executive deck," a subset of your main deck, consisting of only your most critical slides. If you walk into the conference room and are told to keep it short, just click on your executive deck instead of your main deck.

Then you can maintain your composure, your confident pace, and your reputation as an excellent presenter.

Show Your Leadership Presence: Participate in Discussions

Senior managers will get into discussions among themselves, leaving you standing awkwardly at the front of the room, stalled in the middle of your presentation and not knowing how to get it back on track.

If your tendency is to stand there and wait to be told to continue, consider being a bit more proactive.

Consider the possibility of joining the discussion. Of course, you have to be politically sensitive and not barge in where you don't belong. But, don't let your own sense of being lower on the totem pole hinder your engagement. It is, after all, your presentation. And you might very well add something to their discussion that clarifies it immediately, leaving you free to continue and senior management free to appreciate what an outstanding employee they have!

On that same note, presentations to senior management must establish immediate forward momentum and presenters must learn to project confidence.

If you are frequently interrupted or knocked off course by senior management audiences, it might be because you start out tentatively. Build a strong introduction and move quickly into your main material. Even senior managers will get out of the way if they sense a fast moving train moving toward them.

Here are some tips for making a strong first impression and gathering everyone's attention and respect, right from the start:

- Take center stage with confidence. Walk up to the podium, the front of the room, the head of a table, wherever you'll be speaking, without hesitation.

- Connect immediately with unswerving, full-room eye contact. Don't just look at one person in the front.
- Own the geography. Will you stand next to a slide projector, walk around the stage with a microphone?
- Use the "B" key. In a PowerPoint presentation, you don't want slides showing every single second. By using the "B," or blank key, you can blank out the screen and refocus the attention on you and what you are saying. This is a power move! Don't hide behind your slides. People are visually oriented, if there are images or even words on the screen, a substantial portion of their attention will be there, not on you. Take back their attention at important intervals.
- Project clearly. This is a sign of confidence. No one should have to ask you to "speak up."
- Pause regularly, after important points. This allows your audience to absorb what you just said, and it gives you a breather. Pausing also shows confidence, that you are not just barreling along full-speed, hoping to get it over with as quickly as possible.
- Avoid speech fillers and unnecessary qualifiers. Practice until you can eliminate *ums* and *ahs* and *well, you knows* from your speech. Eliminate false starts, stopping mid-sentence, and any words that make you sound less than authoritative.

Presentation Tip: Speak with as much confidence as possible. Act and sound like you expect to be heard; it will increase the likelihood that you *are* heard. Where do you get that confidence? From thorough preparation and methodical practice!

Chapter 10
Talking Tech With Ease & Clarity

"Few things are impossible to diligence and skill." ~ Samuel Johnson, author

When a technical expert needs to give a presentation to a lay audience or a group without the same level of expertise, the material must be framed and presented in an entirely different way. It must be simplified, clarified, and brought to life, to avoid a gaping disconnect between the speaker and the audience.

Although this might sound like a completely different presentation issue than the ones we've been discussing in previous chapters, the solutions are basically the same: thorough preparation along with taking the attitudes, expertise, and needs of your audience into consideration.

What Are Their Priorities?

The way you put together your presentation has everything to do with your audience. If you are presenting to senior management in your own company, you would design something very different than if you are a researcher speaking at a medical conference, or an engineer speaking at a community fundraiser.

When making a technical presentation, remember the WIIFT? at all times: What's in it for them? Why do they need to know this information, what is their interest, how might it inspire or move them, what might they do with it? This will inform the amount and type of technical details you present, the language you use, and the perspective you use when presenting.

Here are two different examples:

- **Presenting to management:** As a technically oriented presenter, you may be focused on the specifics of what you developed, how it evolved, and what the challenges were in your day-to-day work. In other words, the technical details. But management will be more focused on the destination, not the challenges inherent in getting there. In other words, they're thinking as end users. *Will we be able to do this? Will our customers be able to do that? What will the report look like?* You'll need to tailor your presentation to give them what they need to know from their perspective and their positions.

- **Presenting to your industry or another lay audience:** Perhaps you have been working on an ongoing project to bring clean water to certain areas in Africa. You are presenting your findings at a medical convention. Remember, the medical professionals at this conference will not be interested in the details of well or reservoir construction that you find so fascinating. They will not understand any engineering jargon, so keep it to the barest bones. They will be more interested in hearing your findings on how bringing in clean water affected the community's health. Always focus your presentation with the audience's interests in mind.

Bottom line in any technical presentation: What you're most interested in might not be what they're most interested in. To succeed with a non-technical audience, you must understand this difference and commit to delivering presentations that will *satisfy the audience's priorities.*

Table the Tech Talk & Give It to Them in Plain English

You may not think of yourself as multi-lingual, but in fact, you are. You speak *tech* (i.e. computers, science, medicine, analytics, etc.). You may be more fluent expressing yourself and your ideas in this language than you are in standard English. But when you present to people who don't share your technical background, *your success depends on using plain English.* It depends on translating your ideas, your theories, your research, your specifications, and your work into language others can easily understand. And yes, that will likely mean taking out a lot of it, perhaps even the parts you find most exciting.

> **Presentation Pitfall:** You might not realize how much you use jargon. Have a non-technical person listen to you rehearse your presentation and point out any jargon or tech-talk that they do not understand.

Master the Art of the Analogy

When presenting technical information to non-technical audiences, it's likely you'll be describing things that are foreign to them. It's imperative that you make a connection with something they already know; analogies are perfect for this purpose.

For example: Information technology specialists often refer to plumbing when talking about bandwidth. They talk about different size pipes and the amount of liquid (aka data) that can flow through them. Non-technical audiences may be clueless about the technology involved, but they understand plumbing well enough to make the connection and grasp bandwidth.

Become a master of analogies in your field. Draw from day-to-day life to create your comparisons, things everyone is familiar with. When you come up with a good analogy, add it to your repertoire. Use it when you face your next non-technical audience.

Diagram and Demonstrate

You undoubtedly have heard the old saying "seeing is believing." It could also be said that "seeing is understanding." YouTube has become a worldwide phenomenon in part because so many people prefer to see something, instead of reading about it or just listening to somebody talk about it.

You can talk about something all night and only generate the smallest speck of understanding; but put up a diagram or draw something on a flip chart and light bulbs appear above the heads of your audience members. "OK, I get it. I see what you're talking about."

This phenomenon also holds true with demonstrations. Show them what the software does. Demonstrate the engineering solution with a working model.

Be That Unusually Good Technical Presenter

Technical presenters who are good at connecting with non-technical audiences are rare, but you can become a part of this group by:

- keeping your audience's level of knowledge and priorities in mind
- dropping the jargon and translating into plain English
- being a master of analogy, so your audience can really "get it"
- diagramming and demonstrating
- remembering you are selling yourself and your ideas

Chapter 11

Virtual Presentations: Gaining the eVantage

"Communication -- the human connection -- is the key to personal and career success." – Paul J. Meyer, author and entrepreneur

How do you engage audience members and adjust your presentation to their reactions and needs … when you can't make eye contact or read their body language?

As technology continues to proliferate at the speed of light, ePresentations have become more commonplace. There are various challenges that are unique to ePresentations, and I'm not talking about technical issues!

The biggest challenge is that presenters might feel like they are speaking into a void, holding back their urge to say, "Hello. Is anybody listening?"

Yes, it takes extra care and energy to engage and connect with your remote audiences – double entendre deliberate – when you can't see them and their reactions.

Do you believe you can effectively engage a virtual audience? If you believe virtual presenting is bound to be inferior, your presentation will also be inferior. You'll set your standards low and deliver accordingly.

Remember that, just in case you need to make a bit of attitude adjustment while we discuss accepting and overcoming the differences between face-to-face presentations and ePresentations.

I encourage you to use a simple slide design – keep the visuals visual. That means …

- Use one background template for all slides – either light text on a dark background or vice versa.
- Wherever possible, use charts, diagrams, pictures and

other graphics – they really help convey your information and better grab participants' attention. There are many websites that offer royalty-free, low-cost images; two are: istockphoto.com and dollarphotoclub.com.

- When using bullets, be sure you use a build.
- Use only one font style; the best for webinar slide readability is Arial.
- Ensure that you know the screen format on which the audience is viewing your presentation.

Presentation Tip:
If you are the presenter for a group webinar using one feed via a conference room, the screen format may well be widescreen (16:9 ratio vs. the standard projection system format of 4:3.) You'll lose key information if your presentation is set for 4:3 and shown on a 16:9.

There are four key best practices that can ensure your next virtual presentation is effective:

1) Know the meeting software's tools and use them:

The fact is, you can do some cool technological tricks online, so why not take advantage of this? Familiarize yourself completely with the Web conferencing system (WebEx, GoToMeeting, Adobe Connect, etc.) that you are using and its capabilities. Hold audience member attention and add action to your presentation with highlighting, drawing, a white board and other tools.

Other technical advantages of ePresentations include:

- ability to conduct instant surveys of audience members, with results available in minutes
- live chat features
- most Web conferencing software allows participants to be broken down into teams, so they can communicate with each by using "breakout rooms" – this prevents interrupting others

- recording and archiving presentations to be viewed at a later date

2) Continuously encourage participants to:

- use the chat feature to ask questions, respond to your questions, and make comments
- raise their electronic hands when they want to verbalize a question
- respond to polling questions that you have set up using the polling feature
- type on the slides during brainstorming segments

These kinds of features keep your participants active and ensure connection.

3) Reach out to and call on people more: (This refers to virtual meetings with people you know, or you at least know their names.) In a virtual situation, to keep engagement and gauge where your attendees' minds are, you'll have to reach into the void to connect much more frequently than you would face-to-face. "John, what's your opinion on that?" "Mary, I know you've had this kind of situation before. How have you handled it in the past?"

Yes, you are putting people on the spot by soliciting opinions and asking for input, so be cautious about the kind of questions you are asking. Don't embarrass them with questions they could potentially stumble on.

Regularly calling on people will keep everyone in your audience on their toes ... in case they get called. Some experts fear virtual meetings negatively impact participants' energy levels, eliminating the camaraderie and excitement that an in-person meeting can achieve. Compensate for this by frequently urging audience participation.

4) Increase the animation in your voice:

When others can't see you, your voice becomes your most important tool. It's the only thing others have to "read" your attitude, and the only thing you have to hold their attention.

When you practice a virtual presentation, ask yourself:
- Do you sound engaged? Conversational?
- Would anybody listening to you know that you are really excited about the topic?
- Or, does your voice have low energy and sound bored?

Record one of your practice sessions. You may be surprised at how flat you sound.

Another element to consider when you present virtually is incorporating a webcam to allow for live streaming video while you talk. This visual element is another factor that increases connectivity for a remote audience. They can relate better to a face than just a voice. As I said earlier in the book, the power of visual cues when speaking – even virtually -- can't be underestimated.

Virtual Presentation Tips
- Use a headset and stand while presenting.
- Gesture toward your computer (even if they can't see you doing so).
- Check yourself out in a mirror to make sure you're smiling; the smile comes across in your voice.

Guaranteed, if you do these three things, you'll sound more alive than if you just sit in front of the screen motionless.

Eight Ideas to Improve *Your* Next Online Event

- **Get off to a fast start.** Nothing is more boring than staring at a screen while emcees and facilitators drone on and on about their day, how happy they are to be doing the webinar, etc.

- **Spend no more than two minutes to introduce your event, covering the features of your Web conferencing software.** Then move aside and let the main presenter start. This will give your event a fast-paced feel that will keep participants engaged and tuned in.

- **Keep it short.** Virtual events that are 60 to 90 minutes in length are the most effective. If your program requires more time, consider breaking it into segments delivered over a period of days or weeks. As with a face-to-face presentation, identify the three or four key messages you want to impart, and build your presentation around them. In a 90-minute program, this will give you enough time to interact with audience members -- asking questions and answering any they may have.

- **Make the webinar interactive.** To compensate for limited attention spans, change slides every 60 to 90 seconds. Also, interact with participants every 3 to 5 minutes, to keep them involved. This is where you use the annotation tools: polls, text chat, hand raising, etc. You can also do this by including video, two-way audio via VOIP, and stories and examples to support your ideas.

- **Test, test and retest.** Once your event is staged and ready to go, make sure you test the "links" that will be sent to your registered participants. Failure to check links and phone numbers are the most common mistakes made in producing Web events, and are completely preventable.

- **On the day of the presentation, set up two computers, one with your presenter's view and another logged on as an audience member.** This gives you a much better sense of what your participants are experiencing. Slides that are slow may display quickly for the audience. This will also allow you to check the formatting and appearance of your visuals from the participant's perspective.

- **Practice, practice, practice.** If you're not a pro at presenting virtually, I highly recommend not only practicing your delivery, but setting up an actual dry run using the exact platform you will be using for the live event – WebEx, GoToMeeting, etc. This practice should use the actual deck you intend to use, as well as incorporate your practice using annotation tools, and any other "bells and whistles" of the platform. Enlist the help of a colleague, who can sign in and allow you to pass control of the slides to him or her – much like what could happen during a live event.

- **Use a specialist.** For live events with a large audience, use an "online specialist" or producer to answer questions submitted by the audience while you are presenting. The barriers to participation are low in an online event, so you can expect to receive more questions and comments than in a typical face-to-face presentation. Using a specialist means that everyone who asks a question will get a personalized response. This also allows you to stay focused on delivering your key points without being distracted by a high volume of questions.

Chapter 12

Presenting with Tablets & Other High-Tech Gadgets

"It's supposed to be automatic, but actually you have to push this button." ~John Brunner, author

Although I've mentioned many times not to start making slides before you know your main goals, themes, and messages, don't take that to mean I'm against technology. It's still essential in the creation and delivery of a phenomenal presentation.

Modern technology can be an invaluable and innovative aid. Let's start with tablets. You can use your iPad or tablet to hold your notes, to keep track of the time, or to show your slides or photos if you are presenting during a small meeting.

Using your tablet is visually pleasing, interactive, and "greener" than paper. You can stand it up on the table or pass it around.

However, the tablet does have some potential disadvantages:

- It takes the focus off you
- Possible loss of momentum and eye contact while navigating
- Logistical risks (hit off button by mistake, power dies)
- Delays in opening apps and websites

Before starting, make sure your device is fully charged and ready, the screen clean and unlocked, and any apps you need are ready to go.

Also, make sure the time before it blanks out is long enough to allow for discussion on each slide. Otherwise, the screen may go to black automatically in the middle of your presentation. Go to "settings" and turn off your screen lock function to prevent this from happening.

Presentation Tech Tip for iPads: Flipping through your slides by hand can be distracting to an audience, especially if it takes you a while to find the one you're looking for. But by using Apple's Keynote and turning your iPhone into a remote with the Keynote Remote app, you can move around and give touch-free presentations.

If you are using your iPad or other tablet in face-to-face presentations, remember the Three Ts:

- Touch (to bring up the information or slide you want)
- Turn (the device toward your audience)
- Talk (explain what they are looking at)

Always combine your use of technology with a focus on the audience. Do they need more time with a slide? Are they fidgeting from too much back and forth with your tablet?

Be ready to interact, make eye contact, and engage the audience members so you can hold their attention.

If you aren't that familiar with your device, it's a smart idea to practice navigating with it, pulling up apps, and speaking about your slides.

> **Presentation Tech Tip:** Turn on the Manual Do Not Disturb mode to stop notifications from appearing on the device in the middle of your presentation.

Of course, apps change all the time, but these are 10 excellent ones for presentations:

- **Pages:** Apple's basic word processor for writing out your presentation notes.
- **Keynote:** Keynote allows you to create slides.
- **Office HD:** Create word processing files, a slide deck, or spreadsheet.
- **Noteshelf:** Hook this note-taking app up to a projector

and screen, write in real time, create an instant white board! Perfect when you want to involve the audience, get their ideas and feedback, and show it to everyone. You'll need an Apple adapter to plug into the projector.

- **GoodReader®:** Store video, PDFs, slides, etc., then bring them up and play or view them with a click.
- **Evernote:** Take pictures, notes, or any kind of information and store it for future use. Great for ideas that come to you during the preparation stage.
- **Dropbox:** Great for moving large files around and storing them in the cloud, so as not to take up too much real estate on your device.
- **Presentation Clock:** Keep yourself on track and make sure you aren't running over time.
- **Prompster Pro™:** This teleprompter app costs $10, but will be invaluable if you are giving the type of presentation that needs to be read, word for word.
- **2Screens Presentation Expert:** Can be used with an iPhone remote for viewing slideshows, documents or taking on-screen notes. It also can turn the iPhone into an on-screen laser pointer.

PowerPoint Alternatives

Do you have a love-hate relationship with the most popular presentation software on the planet? In 2012, *Bloomberg Business Week* reported PowerPoint had captured 95 percent of the presentation software market, and approximately 350 PowerPoint-based presentations are given every second! That doesn't mean you have to run with the PowerPoint pack, though.

Haiku Deck (Web, iOS): This program stresses the use of art and imagery, making it a must for designers. A bonus—the 35 million pieces of free stock art to go with six included themes.

Prezi (Cloud-based): If you are looking for innovative visuals, Prezi has what *PCMag* called an "animated visual feast unlike the usual boring set of bullet points." The downside: you can only make Prezis that are public. The entire presentation is on one giant slide—you just jump from spot to spot.

SlideDog (Windows): Oh you, SlideDog (get it?). Supports multiple kinds of presentation files and other formats (PDFs, Prezi files, video, images). Drag them into SlideDog, and reorder them for a presentation playlist that can play in sequence or as you need them.

If you like technology, you already know innovative new tools are always showing up in the market. A Google search will hook you up with the latest and greatest in presentation technology.

Regardless of the technology you choose, make sure you practice with it and know how to use all of its features, so that it doesn't distract you or your audience from your message.

Also, keep in mind that iPads, other tablets, and additional tech gadgets, won't ever replace a fabulous presenter and a well-crafted message. They are just additional tools that can help you present more effectively.

Chapter 13
Delivery Styles & Techniques

So far, I've given you techniques to plan, prepare and practice your presentation. There are times, however, that you will be asked to speak at the spur of the moment, or required to write out your presentation and use a teleprompter.

Here are details about different types of delivery styles and how to be successful using each.

Extemporaneous Style

Most presentations fall into this category. A good extemporaneous speech may sound off-the-cuff, but it is not. This is the type of presentation we've been talking about throughout the book: thoughtfully planned, prepared and practiced ahead of time. These are polished presentations which may be given many times, but should never be exactly the same. You may use an outline or notes, but the speech isn't written out or memorized.

Impromptu Style

Also known as "off-the-cuff," impromptu speeches are given on the spur of the moment. Believe it or not, solid practice for planned presentations can also help your confidence with impromptu speeches.

Occasions for impromptu talks include meetings when you were not previously informed that you would be speaking, or when you are asked to give a status report, comment on a proposal, or just share your opinion about the topic under discussion. Many presentations are impromptu, and you can be prepared to present even when you haven't had any advance notice.

The secret?

Relax and let your knowledge of the subject work for you. If you are going to a meeting, you will probably know the topic, so even if no one has asked you to speak, you can still come prepared. After all, why wouldn't you prepare?

When you know your subject well, it's easier to relax and speak. If you even suspect you may be asked for an opinion, do some homework on the topic.

For example: You are going to a meeting where the topic is downsizing in your department, and you are fairly certain your opinion will be solicited since you are a mid-level manager. Now is the time to jot down your thoughts and be prepared. If you are asked to speak, you're ready. If someone else speaks first, you'll be able to agree or disagree and *give your reasons why.*

Here are some benefits of mastering impromptu speaking. It provides...
- an opportunity to shine and impress colleagues and perhaps your boss
- a lead-in to brainstorming sessions resulting in new ideas
- a chance to be heard -- if you have very strong opinions on a topic

Presentation Tip: Critical skills for presenting off-the-cuff information include being succinct, concise, and to the point.

Dos and don'ts for impromptu speaking:

- Don't apologize or make excuses for not being prepared.
- Don't just give your point of view and a reason, and leave it at that.
- Do give an example.
- Do restate your position. After hearing your reasons and examples, your position will have more validity and you will sound confident and solid, someone to be

listened to!
- Don't ramble. It annoys everyone, and makes it sound like you don't really know what you're trying to say.

With some **PREP,** being asked your opinion at a meeting doesn't have to be awkward, embarrassing, or downright terrifying. PREP is a simple pneumonic device to help you master impromptu speaking.

PREP has four steps, but before you get into them, remember to pause, take a breath, and gather your wits about you.

- **P**oint of view: Begin answering the question by giving your point of view, position or perspective. This shows clarity.
- **R**easons: Explain why you support that position, with all the necessary facts and figures at your disposal.
- **E**xamples/**E**xplanations: The more personal and powerful, the better. Use whatever you can to define and reinforce your position.
- **P**oint of view: Wrap it all up by restating your position.

For example, you may be asked, "Which of these three project options do you think will be most successful for us?"

- (Point of view) Pause first. "I believe Project B is the best option."
- (Reasons) "It will be the easiest and most cost effective to implement."
- (Examples/Explanations) "Several clients reported how thrilled they were that we were able to finish the project in less time and under budget, so I believe they would also be inclined to support Project B." Or, "We did a similar project last year, and it took only 60 days when we thought it would be 90. Also, the project ran 7% under budget."
- (Point of view) "With that in mind, I definitely believe Project B is the way to go."

Using PREP will have an enormous impact on your listeners. You will sound credible, well organized, logical, and best of all, concise. Practice your PREP whenever you can.

You want this model to be so second nature, you can easily and automatically slide into it the minute you're asked to speak. Practice on the phone, in e-mail, and any time you can in day-to-day conversations.

What if you are asked not for an opinion, but just for information?

In this case, remember the classic, three-part template for a message.

Intro → Body → Close

If you're completely caught off-guard, don't panic. Again, pause, take a deep breath.

Use what's called the non-committal introduction. It gives you a bit of time because you don't try to get to the point right away. Give your scrambling brain a chance to catch up by limiting yourself to some background or set-the-scene thoughts.

For example, you're asked about the status of Project B.

You might start out with: "As you all know, Project B started about a year ago. It had a small team to begin with but has grown significantly." Just those two sentences—which commit you to nothing—can be enough to get your brain cells in gear and pull up the facts you need. Make sure your opening remarks are directly related to the question asked, and don't say, "Uh. Oh. Let me think. I'm really not prepared."

Next, move into the body of your comments, which should feature the information you've been specifically asked for. As with a planned presentation, limit yourself to a maximum of three main, important points.

For your conclusion, let listeners know you're done. This is hardly ever done, instead many speakers keep rambling on until they run out of things to say. Sum it up succinctly: "Overall, the Project B is right on schedule and we look forward to delivering the final report."

Expromptu Style

A combination of extemporaneous and impromptu, the expromptu speech is prepared ... but not practiced. Unfortunately, this happens too often in corporate America, when people wait too long to prepare, and then run out of time to practice. (Of course, that would never be you!)

You might also be asked to give a presentation at a meeting or conference. You will have some notice, a few minutes to a few hours, so take some time to put your thoughts together, even though you have no time to practice.

You might still have time to write an opening sentence that will set you up to make your points. Use notes to help organize your thoughts. Write a closing sentence to end your presentation. Your success as an expromptu speaker depends on how well you gather and organize your thoughts.

Manuscript Style

This speech is written down and read word for word to the audience. It is widely used in the scientific community, where technical papers requiring exact wording are first submitted for approval and once accepted, they are read by the author.

Politicians and many CEOs use manuscript speeches, as do people presenting something with a teleprompter. The key to success is to write for the ear, not for the eye. Make it conversational.

This format ensures exact adherence to a timetable, essential when each speaker has a limited amount of time available for his or her presentation. You can use visual aids with a manuscript speech; that will make it more interesting for the audience.

Unless you have to use the manuscript style, it is best to avoid it. If you have material that has to be presented exactly as written, do so, but try to be more spontaneous with the rest of the speech.

Tips for reading a manuscript presentation:

- Use the scope technique – slide your thumb and pointer finger down the page, scoping one section at a time. This will help you to find your place after you look up at the audience.
- The manuscript must be easy to read.
- Use sentence case.
- Underline key words, spaces to pause, etc.
- Practice!

You might think a manuscript presentation would be much easier and not require any practice; after all, you are only reading it. In fact, they require a great deal of practice to sound conversational and spontaneous, and to keep your audience awake and engaged.

Sometimes a manuscript presentation may use the teleprompter. Here are four pointers for effectively using a teleprompter when speaking:

- **Remember to smile –** Don't fall into the trap of focusing on reading your presentation, at the expense of remembering to smile from time to time – which kills your connection to audience members.

- **"Work" the camera –** Teleprompters let you directly gaze into a camera to connect with audience members. Make sure you "work" the camera by locking your eyes straight ahead and pretending the lens is a person. If you look away frequently the remote viewer begins to question your integrity/honesty of material.

- **Use non-verbal communication –** I've already discussed how gestures are key to a presenter's success. Speakers who use teleprompters still need to incorporate appropriate gestures.

- **Practice & then practice again –** Practice makes permanent. Practice out loud alone and with others. Record yourself if you can, and tweak your manuscript for any areas in which you stumble.

Memorized Style

Unless you are a professional actor who can memorize speeches, and make them sound like you just came up with the thoughts, forget about memorized style presentations. Most people cannot memorize every word they have written.

The most painful speaker to watch is one who has written a speech, thinks he or she has it memorized gets up to the lectern, and forgets it. Ouch!

Even if you could memorize your speech, it's still not a good idea. If you get stuck, you'll be completely lost. As a speaker, you depend on cues from people in the audience to guide your delivery, adapting it when necessary to meet their needs. It's just about impossible to do this with a memorized presentation.

The 5 Styles of Delivery	
Impromptu	Speeches given on the spur of the moment
Extemporaneous	Given when you have the opportunity to prepare and practice
Manuscript	Given when very exact wording is required
Memorized	Used when you say the presentation the same way each time you give it
Expromptu	You have some time to prepare your thoughts ahead of time, but no time to practice

Chapter 14
Delivery Dynamics: The Visual Elements

"Clothes and manners do not make the man; but, when he is made, they greatly improve his appearance." ~Henry Ward Beecher, Abolitionist, Novelist

You can have a fabulous presentation – good content that is organized – with well-designed slides and still fall flat on your face. Why?

Two words: Poor delivery.

The audience members' perception of you is formed instantly, taking into account three elements of delivery:

- Visual
- Vocal
- Verbal

The visual aspect encompasses your body language, facial expressions, grooming and dress.

The vocal aspect includes the pitch of your voice, and also the passion you project.

The verbal aspect is what you actually say; the words you use to get your message across.

Let's first focus on the visual elements of your presentation.

Your appearance, body language and general demeanor cause everyone in your audience to form immediate impressions about you before you even open your mouth — whether they are consciously aware of it or not.

If this first impression is *not* a positive one, it will be hard to compensate for it, no matter what you say and no matter how well you say it. Since your visual element has the most initial impact, it is important that you properly prepare yourself to show your audience a positive visual message.

Dress for Speaking Success

Dress codes have loosened up over the years. There is no universally "correct" way to dress. It very much depends on the industry, region, season and role of the presenter. The real point is that dress should be intentional – not what happens to be clean in the closet that day.

You might find this superficial or unfair, but how you look can -- and does -- color how people hear you and respond to you. If you've done your homework and researched the audience, you can choose clothing that will enhance your presentation and be appropriate for the occasion.

A general guideline as a presenter is to dress one step above the audience members. It is a sign of respect. If you are wearing a jacket, you can always take it off. Regardless of what you wear, your grooming must be impeccable. Ill-fitting, rumpled clothes that are missing buttons are an indication (a good one) that you don't pay attention to details ... and details are important!

The main thing to remember? Don't wear anything distracting. Here are some general guidelines, keeping in mind that some business environments are very casual.

Women ...

No mini-skirts, low-cut tops, or skin-tight anything. Presentations do not fall under the oft-quoted maxim, "If you've got it, flaunt it." The opposite holds true.

So, nix the chandelier earrings, jangling bracelets, spike-heeled dominatrix boots, leggings, or anything else wild or over-the-top. You want them talking about your brilliant presentation, not your brilliantly colored lips or way too revealing clothing.

Wardrobe Tips for Women

- Check to see there are no runs in stockings, and carry

an extra, "emergency" pair.
- Shoes should be conservative, with low- to mid-sized heels.
- Jewelry should not clang or dangle.
- Sweaters should not cling, and blouses should not be low-cut
- Find out which colors look great on you and wear them. If you are unsure, it's worthwhile to consult a professional image or color consultant.

Men ...

Nothing rumpled. Make sure your shirts are tucked in, your pants are long enough to cover the tops of your shoes, and speaking of shoes — no sneakers! If you're clueless about clothes, find a mentor to advise you.

In short, err on the side of conservative, unless you work in the fashion, entertainment or advertising industries, which have much more latitude.

Wardrobe Tips for Men

When wearing "business professional"...
- A suit demonstrates more authority than a sports coat or blazer. However, if you are in a warm-weather climate, and many members of the audience are wearing short-sleeve shirts or dressing more casually, a suit may be too formal.
- White or light-blue shirts are always appropriate, along with silk ties, high-rise socks, and polished, dark leather shoes.

Dress Tips for Everyone

- Make sure your clothes fit properly. Nothing is more important than clean, pressed, well-fitting attire.
- Dark colors such as navy blue, gray, and black communicate power and authority.
- If you wear glasses, save the tinted lenses for

weekends. People want to see your eyes when you speak.

- The day of your presentation is not the time for new shoes, unless you have broken them in first. You don't want to find yourself standing in front of a group with a pained expression because your feet hurt.
- Use a full-length mirror to check yourself, front and back. Clothing that fits poorly will distract from what you have to say. Audience members may remember your split seam or baggy pants instead of the points you are making.

> **Presentation Tip for Your Wardrobe:** When speaking at a conference, ask the organizer the color of the backdrop. If it's navy blue, and you show up in a navy blue suit -- no matter how well cut or stylish -- you will virtually disappear. When unsure of what to wear, ask the person who has scheduled you to speak, or talk to others in the company.

Eye Contact

Eye contact is a way of connecting with your audience members. It makes a presentation more personal. It also helps you "read" their reaction. If you sense boredom, you'll know to pick up the pace. If you sense enthusiasm, it can help to pump you up. If they appear confused, you can stop and open for questions.

Start with a familiar or friendly face. The general rule of thumb is to finish a short thought, phrase or idea (approximately 3 to 5 seconds) before moving your eyes in a random zigzag pattern throughout the room on to the next person. Don't move on in the middle of a sentence or idea – hold the eye connection and finish the thought.

Rather than a two-eyed stare, look at one eye or the other, or above or below the eyes. If anyone appears uncomfortable with eye contact – usually indicated by avoiding your eye contact -- glance at the person only briefly before moving on.

Facial Expressions

Are you aware of your usual facial expressions? If you're feeling brave and determined to master public speaking, try this: Put a mirror on your desk for one week. Watch your face when you're on the phone. Do you make any artificial, unfriendly, or deadpan expressions? Do you squint, frown, chew your lip, or make strange faces?

Videotape your presentation. Watch to see if you've smiled enough and in appropriate places. If not, write reminder notes to yourself in the margin of your speech or just practice smiling beforehand.

Once you become aware of habitual expressions that may not send the message you want, it will be easier to eliminate them. Practice smiling and looking pleasant. That's how you want to look during your presentations. It isn't easy to speak and smile at the same time, but it *is* important to have an animated expression during your presentation. Make it congruent with your message. Be careful not to "over smile." You may appear insipid or phony.

Body Language While Standing

Have you ever seen a speaker sway? It's a distraction that can detract from even the most interesting presentation. Your posture and the way you conduct yourself on the platform or in front of the room is an important part of your presentation. You want the audience to see that you are relaxed and in control.

Comfortable movements will relax both you and your audience. Pacing is distracting. Instead, use your movements to establish contact with your audience. Take 2 to 3 steps, then stay and "visit," pause there, speak a bit, and then return to your place in front. Movement should be intentional.

Getting physically closer to your audience increases attention and interest. It also encourages a response if you are asking questions. The accepted public distance zone is 12 to 25 feet. In smaller group situations, you can approach within a social distance of 4 to 12 feet primarily, and occasionally get as close as 18 inches to 4 feet. Avoid blocking the screen or being behind people. No one likes people at their back.

> **Presentation Tip:** Hold your head high, chin up. This gives you the aura of being in control; whereas chin down connotes acquiescence.

Another visual element, posture, is also important. What does your body language say about how you feel?

Mom really was looking out for your future when she told you to stand up straight. Body language is read subconsciously, and impressions are formed from it. If you slump or slouch, that might send a message to your audience members that you'd prefer not to send.

If you didn't listen to Mom, it's not too late ...

To evaluate your posture, first look at yourself on video or in photographs. Need improvement? Try these two posture tips:

- Try standing with your feet about 6 to 8 inches apart, parallel to each other with toes pointed straight ahead. Flex your knees and put your weight on the balls of your feet. Standing in this position will stop any swaying or rocking motion and will diminish any distracting heel movements.
- Put your arms loosely by your sides – or pretend that you are reaching for your back pockets; that will throw your shoulders back.

Now your shoulders are over your hips, your back is lengthening and widening and your posture is straight.

What to Do When Presenting While Standing

Good posture; feet balanced; arms resting at side, ready to use

Using gestures to look animated

Open gestures, looking confident

Effective gestures and good posture project confidence and competence – and the response you get from your audience will let you know when you've succeeded.

How can you get the hang of natural, organic gestures? The fact is that practiced gestures can look stiff and stilted. But they don't have to. It's all about the amount of practice. Do it till they feel (and look) comfortable and natural to you.

Pay attention to how you are gesturing when you are talking to friends and telling a story. If you are pantomiming the message, the gestures will flow naturally.

Practice Exercise: Stand in front of a full-length mirror. Get into a comfortable stance, as described above. Now practice a variety of gestures. What *feels* uncomfortable (because it's new) may *look* terrific. What *feels* comfortable may *look* sloppy or fidgety. Practice your gestures three times a week for one minute at a time. Within a month or two, your natural gestures will be more open and fluid. Also, pay attention to your gestures when you are in casual conversation – what are you doing to emphasize a point?

> **Presentation Tip:** Observe passionate speakers. How are they using gestures? You will note that your energy will be greater when you are gesturing.

Perhaps one of the most common speaking stances is arms crossed over the chest. If you're not feeling relaxed or confident, you might take this body posture without even realizing it. The reality is that this stance makes the speaker look defensive. By facing audience members with your arms crossed, you are closing yourself to them, and they will sense this. Since your objective is to communicate with openness and sincerity (isn't it?), you want to make open gestures to reinforce what you are saying.

What about putting your hands in your pockets? Nervous presenters often use this gesture to keep their shaking hands out of sight, and often wind up jingling their keys or the change in their pocket, without realizing it. I once saw a speaker who couldn't get his hands back out again ... and wound up spilling the contents of his pockets as he tried to release his hands.

Talk about an embarrassing moment!

Body Language Don'ts When Presenting While Standing

Hands on hips	Reading notes	Praying position	Arms crossed	Parade rest	Fig leaf	Pointed finger

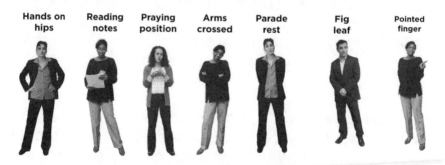

Weak twirling motions with your hands or wagging your fingers when making a point also indicates your unease to the audience.

Clasping your hands into a folded position (like you're praying), is another gesture to eliminate. It tightens your upper body and pulls in your energy instead of releasing it.

Since gestures can be so problematic, why use them at all? Why not just develop a nice, neutral stance, and stick with it? Why? Because after a few short minutes, this will look unnatural.

Gestures help you to emphasize important points during your presentation. They reinforce what you're saying with a visual message. Of course, the most effective gestures are the spontaneous ones that arise from what you're thinking and feeling. They help the audience members relate to you and what you are telling them – in essence, pantomime the message.

A speaker who uses natural, appropriate movement is much more appealing and persuasive than someone standing behind the lectern, hands rigidly clasped in front (or behind) his or her body.

Have you ever watched an evangelist on television using wide, sweeping gestures while speaking? These gestures are effective, because they include everyone, making viewers feel a part of things -- even though they are watching from their own home.

As a presenter in a business setting, you are nothing like a television evangelist or Broadway performer projecting into the "cheap seats," so use gestures sparingly and only to emphasize points in your presentation.

Body Language While Seated

You're at a meeting and have just been asked for your opinion. You are unprepared, nervous and want to slump down in your seat so no one will notice you. No matter how nervous you are, now is the time to sit up straight in your chair, keep your hands above the table, use gestures and make eye contact.

If you are presenting while seated, you want to look energized and confident. No leaning, slouching or appearing too relaxed. Don't sprawl! Also, don't swivel the chair. Proper seated posture when presenting (or if you want to look good at a meeting) is sitting with your spine straight, your feet flat on the floor and hands open on the table.

While you're trying to collect your thoughts, open by paraphrasing the question you have just been asked. This provides a brief amount of time to think of what to say. Others at the meeting will be responding to your body language. How you look, gesture, and make eye contact will be influencing their opinions, even before you open your mouth.

Body Language Don'ts When Presenting While Seated

Slouching, keeping hands below table

Arms crossed with no eye contact

Pointing finger

Arms behind head (looks very arrogant)

Looking at the computer monitor then at audience

Knocking over a drink

Multi-tasking

Looking disengaged

Body Language Dos When Presenting While Seated

- Hands above the table
- Gesturing
- Good eye contact
- Animated face
- Smiling

Tip: In order to look taller, be sure that you have raised your chair as much as possible.

Hand, arm, and head movements are visual reinforcements of the words and ideas you're trying to communicate.

Gestures can enhance your presentation or detract from it. Have you ever had a conversation with someone who "talks with their hands?"

Presentation Tip: To avoid embarrassment, empty your pockets of change and keys before presenting.

Gesture Tips:

- Use the upper half of your body, with broad, flowing movements.
- Keep your palms open. Move your arm and hand as a single unit, gesturing up and out toward the audience. Use either one or both arms.
- Vary your gestures; don't use the same motion over and over again. (It starts to look like a quirk and will be highly distracting.)
- Relate the extent of your gestures to the size of your audience. Bigger audiences need bigger gestures.
- Nod and smile to emphasize what you're saying.

I've talked about you as a visual – and believe me, you are more important than any slide deck. But now, let's talk about using the fabulous slides that you have created.

16 Tech-Tested Rules for Using Visual Aids

- **Visual aids should be so simple** the audience grasps the concept in *less than 20 seconds.* If material is complex, do a gradual build – start with an easy-to-understand point and work up to the more complex.

- **Make sure everything is spelled correctly,** especially customers' names and products.

- **Practice with visual aids before your presentation!** If possible, do so onsite, as their equipment might work differently than yours. If renting or borrowing equipment, make sure you are familiar with it before your presentation.

- **Have a copy of your slides --** on a memory stick, which can be used in someone else's computer.

- **Make a list of your slides and number each one.** If you want to skip a few slides, simply hit the number of the slide you want to show, then push "enter." It will go to the slide you selected.

- **Arrive early – get the equipment working and in focus.** This includes your remote control to change slides.

- **Bring (or ensure they are already onsite) any supplies you may need --** extension cords, power surge protectors and cables you might need, duct tape and scissors to secure wires to the floor and walls, so no one will trip.

- **Be sure your laptop/tablet is ready to go --** your device is fully charged and you have its power cord just in case.

- **Carry an auxiliary light with you,** or request one if the room will be darkened.

- **Confirm and test Internet access --** If you are using the Internet, verify that the room has compatible connections for your laptop or WiFi as needed.

- **Visibility is key.** Check the screen's visibility in the corners and the back row of the room. Avoid standing in the light when something is projected on the screen.

- **Stand with the visual aid to your left.** Point with your left hand, which should be closest to the screen. (We read from left to right, so we want to point to the beginning of the sentence.)

- **Explain what the audience is seeing before speaking to its significance**. Don't make visuals so complicated that the audience is still reading while you talk.

- **Touch, turn, talk – meaning, point out where you want the audience to look, but before talking again, turn toward the audience.** Don't talk to the screen, talk to the audience.

- **Verbally transition before showing the next slide, and remember to pause once before clicking on to the next slide,** giving people a chance to look the current one over.

- **If something goes wrong with the visual aids or equipment, turn the machine off and keep going.** Don't waste your valuable presentation time fiddling about with faulty equipment. Remember: The visuals are an aid *for the audience,* not you. You must be able to present without them.

Chapter 15
The Vocal Elements: Tone, Pitch, Volume & Speed

"Words mean more than what is set down on paper. It takes the human voice to infuse them with deeper meaning."
~Maya Angelou

So often I have had speakers say to me, "My topic is boring so my presentation will be boring." My response? "With that attitude, you are probably right."

There are no boring topics – there are only boring speakers! Your job as a speaker is to figure out why the audience needs the information – then present it with passion. Not only do you need to look enthusiastic, you need to sound enthusiastic (it's amazing how the two work together!).

Have you ever considered the sound of your voice? Many of us cringe to hear ourselves on a recording, because any accent, any odd inflection, any unappealing pitch, sounds amplified and awful.

Do I really sound like that, you wonder? Perhaps we are just being overly self-critical. But the way you speak — including whether your voice is high or low, fast or slow, pleasing or jarring -- has an impact on how you are perceived, how much of your presentation people will hear, and your overall success as a speaker.

Think of some famous people who are well known for their voices: Morgan Freeman and James Earl Jones have deep, resonant voices. We love to listen to them.

Fran Drescher, who played the Nanny on TV, had a heavy New York accent and a voice people either loved or hated — it was one of her claims to fame.

Let's take a look at the main factors in your speaking voice, and what can be done to maximize your vocal appeal.

Tone & Pitch

The Huffington Post reported on a study in the following article: "Male CEOs With Deep Voices More Likely To Have Market Success."

As political campaign managers have long known, the study showed that a deep voice is perceived as a favorable leadership quality. People are instinctively more likely to trust a candidate with a deep voice, whether they are aware of it or not.

Male or female, your voice *does* play a big part in audience perception. When stressed, our voices tend to rise, but the deeper the pitch, the longer people will listen to what you have to say. You can learn to gain control over your pitch and bring it into a lower range.

Try this exercise. Repeat the following 10 bullets, each time using a deeper pitch:

- "This is my normal pitch."
- Do.
- Re.
- Me.
- Fa.
- So.
- La.
- Ti.
- Do.
- "This is my normal pitch."

Can you hear a difference between the first and third sentence? It might feel awkward at first, but if you practice this exercise 10 times a day for six weeks, you will have much greater control over your pitch.

If you really have a problem with your voice, and a lot of presenting ahead of you, consider working with a vocal coach, just like the pros!

Volume

Is there anything more irritating than people who speak so softly that they cannot be heard? Yes, those who always sound like they're shouting are equally irritating. Don't irritate your audience in such an unnecessary fashion. Being able to control your volume, and *vary it,* will help you hold the audience's attention. To help you control your volume, *try this exercise:*

Breathe from the diaphragm, and speak as if your voice is hitting the back wall of the room you are in. Breathing from the diaphragm allows more air flow, and will help to avoid a sore throat when projecting.

Fast Talk/Slow Talk

Along with volume, speed of delivery is important to master when presenting. The normal speaking rate is between 160-200 words per minute. This varies throughout the different regions of the United States.

If you speak too rapidly, people cannot absorb your information, and they'll wear themselves out trying to keep up, leaving the presentation exhausted – or worse, they will give up and tune you out! If you speak too slowly, their minds will wander, they'll miss just as much information, and leave bored and disappointed.

How do you know whether your speed is on track or barreling down it?

You can test your regular speaking pace by paying attention to how people respond to you in conversation. If people are always asking you to repeat yourself, you probably talk too fast. If they keep interrupting you, you probably speak too slowly. This feedback can help you determine whether you should speed up or slow down when it is time to present.

Reading aloud also helps to assess your rate. Take 120 to 200 words from a book or magazine, and time yourself as you read them using your normal speaking pace. Based on the results, you will know whether to slow down or speed up your normal rate. Practice every day until comfortable with your new rate of speech.

Presentation Tip: Your speed may need to vary, depending on your audience. You may find regional differences throughout the country. When English isn't a first language, a slower speed is necessary. If your information is very technical, slow down and pause frequently for the audience to grasp the meaning.

Diction

Can you articulate clearly? Many mispronunciation problems are the result of bad diction habits and regional peculiarities. In some areas of the country, it is common to hear the endings of words clipped off or changed, for example: *gonna* for going to, *doin* for doing, *thinkin* for thinking. The problem with this is that it sounds sloppy.

Most pronunciation and diction problems can be corrected by listening to good speakers, asking when you are not sure how to pronounce a word, looking up unfamiliar words in the dictionary or by coaching from a qualified speech instructor.

Emphasis (Punching It!)

When we speak, we tend to emphasize certain words or phrases. In your presentations, emphasize the words and phrases that bring your point home. You can change the meaning of a sentence simply by changing the words you emphasize.

The technique used to emphasize words or phrases in your presentation is called "punching" it. Professional speakers and speech writers underline the words and phrases they want to emphasize.

You can do the same on your own outline and when you practice the presentation, also practice "punching" it.

For example, in this sentence, the emphasis changes the speaker's intent: "When we deal with companies *your* size ..." compared to "When we deal with companies your *size* .... " The reality is that depending which one you emphasize, you can get six different meanings from the one sentence.

Pause to Punctuate

Many people are extremely uncomfortable with silence, particularly when they are speaking before others. Make silence your friend because the pause is as critical in oral language as punctuation is to written language.

When you fill pauses with "and," "uh," "um," "OK" and "you know," it's distracting. It doesn't allow the audience members to think about what you are saying, and it sounds unpolished and amateurish.

I recently heard a psychologist speak. She had an interesting topic and was an attractive presenter — dressed appropriately, excellent body language, natural gestures. But ... none of that could compensate for her one "fatal" flaw.

If this had been a speech, it would be the perfect place for me to stop for a powerful, attention-focusing pause!

Within moments of this psychologist's opening remarks, I found myself counting the "ums" in her speech (just out of curiosity). I stopped at 100.

Pauses are also frequently misused. An effective pause emphasizes what has just been said, or what is to come.

For example, if you are going to announce a decision you have made, or a new product your company is coming out with, your presentation should have pauses for dramatic emphasis: "Our company has developed a way to remove the fat content from foods. This new product, now available in test markets, will change the way the world eats. We call it (dramatic, leave-them-hanging-on-the-edge-of-their-seats pause) Remove."

This brief pause literally sets the stage, focuses attention, and ensures your audience will be "all ears" for whatever comes next.

However, some pauses can hurt your presentation -- pauses that detract from what you are trying to say because they happen at inappropriate times, often when you've forgotten what you wanted to say or lost your place. Thorough preparation and practice should eliminate these awkward silences.

Voice Problems

As I said earlier, a deep, resonant voice, like James Earl Jones or Morgan Freeman, will call attention to itself in a favorable way. We all seem to admire those types of voices. Your voice becomes a problem when it calls attention to itself in an unfavorable way.

Common voice problems include:

• Harshness – unless it is physical in nature, a harsh voice indicates tension and stress. Use relaxation techniques to help eliminate the problem. If your throat is dry, drink warm water with lemon before speaking.

• Nasality – frequently caused by clenched jaws, it can be reduced by opening the mouth wider and using the tongue more firmly.

• Breathlessness – usually caused by insufficient breathing while speaking. Take deeper breaths and release a controlled flow of air.

- High pitch – unless physical in nature, this can be improved with vocal exercises and a conscious effort to speak in your lower vocal range.

Finish with Strength

Does your voice rise at the end of a sentence?

Record the first few lines of your presentation. If your voice goes up at the end of sentences, it will sound as though you are asking a question or are tentative.

If you swallow your last few words, you also reduce the impact of what you're saying. Finish sentences completely, and learn to drop your pitch slightly *while keeping the volume strong.*

Listen to newscasters as they close their broadcasts; most of them use a tag line which they repeat regularly with their volume up and pitch down. Practice this until you are comfortable with the way you sound.

Key Takeaways

The way you say what you say matters. So...

- Vary your volume, rate and pitch.
- Sound enthusiastic ... better yet, BE enthusiastic.
- Enunciate your words clearly and correctly.
- Use pauses for emphasis.
- Demonstrate passion – this is what truly engages an audience.

Chapter 16
Verbal Cues: Choosing Words Wisely

"The definition of genius is taking the complex and making it simple." ~Albert Einstein

Think of a time when you were in the audience and couldn't follow or understand the speaker. Communicating clearly and concisely is always the presenter's goal ... and greatest challenge.

Effective speakers use short, simple sentences that are easy to understand – and sound conversational, so they can connect and influence.

Following the guidelines below will allow you to **clearly communicate** your message.

In general, avoid jargon and acronyms, unless everyone understands them. Talk the way your audience does, using familiar words and concepts. When presenting to a technical group, by all means use technical terms and jargon, but be sure to define them the first time you use them. Don't assume they understand. If you use words or phrases that may have different meanings, be sure to explain your meaning.

Using words effectively will also keep your audience **interested** in your message. Share anecdotes to bring yourself into your listeners' world by relating experiences you may have in common with them. Include colorful language that appeals to the different senses (visual, auditory and kinesthetic). Use analogies and metaphors to paint a picture for your audience members.

Power Robbers & Tag Questions

Unfortunately, too many people unknowingly use "power robbers" which detract from our confidence, authority, professionalism and power. Hedges and qualifiers are also common power robbers. Here are some of the worst offenders:

"I guess,"
"I hope"
"I think"
"probably"
"kinda"
"sorta"
"maybe"
"like"
"you know"

Do these power robbers filter into your speech? Get some feedback, because most people are unaware of how frequently they use them. If you use these, then do so intentionally - not out of habit. After all, are you really guessing?

Which sounds more convincing?

"I guess what I am trying to do is ..."
"I will do..."

You choose!

Passive sentences are also power robbers. For example: "Because of increased client demand, it became necessary to develop my organizational and writing skills."

Active constructions give us more power. For example: "I developed my organizational skills and sharpened my professional writing abilities to better service growing client demands."

The first sentence sounds like the speaker was forced into doing what he didn't really want to do. He sounds like a victim. The second sentence shows his initiative and strong proactive behavior in meeting client needs. Night and day!

> **Persuasive Presentation Tip:** Three strong, persuasive words to include in your presentations are "urge," "recommend," and "suggest." Most statements in business should be you-based. "This is a great new copy machine. Imagine all the benefits to you and your company. I urge you to try it out." Using "you" statements fulfills the other party's ongoing question, WIIFM?

Tag Questions

Tag questions cut your effectiveness off at the knees. I'm referring to those little, not-so-harmless questions people tack on to the end of their sentences. "I think it's a good idea, don't you?" "I know my group's solution to fighting these rumors is a good one, isn't it?"

These little add-ons give the impression you are unsure, insecure, or are looking for approval. The phrase, "isn't it?" at the end of a sentence weakens the entire sentence. This is particularly hazardous in persuasive presentations.

Think about what you really want to say and how you are going to say it. Then say *exactly what you mean — without questioning it.*

You can minimize the effect of power robbers in three ways:

- identify your own tendencies
- correct the behavior
- replace the bad habit with a good one (practice makes natural!)

Presentation Pitfall: Your incorrect pronunciation undermines your ability to influence people.

A friend told the story of a speaker who couldn't, for whatever reason, pronounce the word, "jihad." Instead, he repeatedly said, "jahid." People snickered behind their hands and the point he was trying to make lost all of its power. No one could even remember the point, only the mispronunciation.

People who mispronounce words are thought to be poorly educated, illiterate, or just not very bright. Don't burden yourself with that kind of reputation. If you are unsure about a pronunciation, look it up in the dictionary – or don't use it.

Also avoid:
- Slang
- Foul language
- Undefined acronyms, jargon and buzz words
- Pretentious language
- "To tell you the truth," "To be perfectly honest" (Always be honest and truthful ... no need to say it!)

Mastering the verbal elements of a presentation will give you tremendous confidence, and ensure your presentations are polished and professional.

Key Takeaways

- Use clear, crisp and confident language.
- Avoid hedges and qualifiers.
- Paint pictures with your words; appeal to all senses.
- Learn how to pronounce the words you use.
- If you have a question, ask it.
- If it's a statement, make it.
- Sound conversational.

Chapter 17
Practice!

"Spontaneity is an infinite number of rehearsed possibilities."
– Peter Drucker

Your outline is prepared. Your arguments are well thought out, your main points are well researched, and your entire presentation is logically organized to take your audience members to the conclusion you want them to reach.

Even better, as you read your "final draft" to yourself, it sounds fantastic. Are you ready to present?

Let me ask you another question. Given equally well-prepared materials, what separates the outstanding presenters from the rest?

It's practice -- practicing repeatedly, until they are comfortable, confident, flowing, and able to be spontaneous.

Here's a not-so-little tip: Practicing in your head isn't really practicing. In our heads, we all sound eloquent.

Sure, we've all heard about top athletes who visualize their performance before stepping out on the field, or on the ice, etc. But, I'll bet you've never heard of an athlete who relies solely on that visualization, and doesn't also practice.

We are all quite eloquent in our minds -- masterful, brilliant even. When we speak aloud, however, something entirely different frequently happens. The only way to practice a presentation is aloud.

Remember, practice makes permanent. Perfect practice makes perfect.

Practice tips for presentation mastery:

- **Say it differently.** This helps you keep the spontaneity, and stay calm and confident with any last-minute changes. The goal is to sound conversational, not stiff or memorized. Three to six practices are usually enough to "own" the material.
- **Practice rough spots.** After practicing several times, try practicing just the rough spots. Try those along with your opening and closing statements, key points, and transitions until you are comfortable with them.
- **Practice as you'll present.** If you will be standing, then stand. If you will be seated, sit.
- **Record yourself.** After you have practiced aloud several times. As you listen, ask yourself if you would enjoy this presentation if you were a member of your audience. If you wouldn't, it's time to revise and practice again. Work on your timing.
- **Include visual aids.** During your last few practice sessions, include whatever visual aids or handouts you will use during your presentation. Too many visuals ... or not enough? Make any final adjustments. You also need to be familiar with the equipment you'll use.
- **Do a dress rehearsal.** Set up an area with a similar seating arrangement. Better yet, go to the actual room where you will be presenting. If possible, try to have a live audience or at least one person similar to your real audience. Give your entire presentation, including questions from the "audience." Important: Ask for feedback and make any last-minute corrections. Make sure you can easily see your notes.
- **Technical presentations.** Give complicated or technical presentations to a spouse or a friend similar to your intended audience, to gauge how easy the material is to understand.

Use every opportunity to practice. A perfect time is when you are driving, jogging, skiing, etc. You get the picture!

While practicing, get feedback from others on your 3Vs. They can use the Presentation Analysis Feedback Form below.

Presentation Analysis Feedback Form

VISUAL	VOCAL	VERBAL
(feet, posture, gesturing, chin up, smile, eye contact, visual aids – TTT,* movement, facial expression)	(fillers, pitch, variety, volume, rate, punch, pause, words trailing off, sentences trailing off, rising intonation, diction)	(qualifiers, simple sentences, descriptive buzz words, tag questions, introduction, closing, main points, transition phrases)

*Touch, Turn, Talk

Presentation Tip: Running over your allotted times or rushing the end of your speech to get everything in can destroy the overall impact of your presentation. Practice also can help to get the timing right.

Follow this formula:

- **75% rule of thumb:** If your presentation will not include interruptions, interaction or questions (such as a keynote), prepare and practice your presentation to go for 75% of the allotted time (e.g.: 45 minutes for a 60-minute time frame). Almost inevitably, the presentation will end up taking the full hour. The worst thing that could happen is that you will be finished early -- and no one complains about that! You can also allow time for questions at the end without rushing.
- **50% rule of thumb:** If your presentation will include some questions and interaction, plan, prepare and practice the presentation to last for 50% of the allotted time (30 minutes for a 60-minute presentation).
- **25% rule of thumb:** If your presentation is highly interactive, like in a training session, sales situation, or when speaking to senior leaders, limit your talk to 25% of the allotted time.

Presentation Reminder: Don't forget to categorize your material as must know, should know and could know. That way, you can take out material throughout the practice session, and even during the actual delivery.

Use a clock during practice and write notes on your outline about the amount of time each section actually represents -- not how much time you think it will take.

Practice on site

As I said, if possible, practice your presentation in the room where you will be giving it. Don't be shy about requesting a table for your notes. I don't advocate using a lectern – it separates you from your audience. If you must use one, step out from behind the lectern and move closer to the audience. If you are nervous and need to refer to your notes, walk behind it again when you feel the need. You could also put your notes on a music stand or table. Speakers who spend their entire presentation behind the lectern seem aloof, don't they?

If you're short, you might wind up staying behind the lectern because it has a riser to make you tall enough to be seen. A better choice is to walk forward and stand closer to your audience members. This will help you establish a good rapport.

If you are forced to stand behind the lectern because that's where the microphone is, consider requesting the use of a wireless (lavaliere) microphone or ... buy your own. Of course, familiarize yourself with its use well in advance of your presentation so you are not fumbling around feeling foolish. Also, make sure you know how turn it off and on with ease.

Presentation Tip: Remember to turn the microphone off as you leave the platform, so any private remarks you may make are not overheard by the audience (I'd share the details of the time a female presenter left her mic on when she went to the bathroom, but I think you get the idea. Do you think her audience was paying attention to her remarks after that?).

On the day of your presentation:

- Arrive early and check the room; locate electrical outlets, and test them.
- Distribute any handouts.
- Test your equipment. Know how to contact the audio-visual assistants.
- If necessary, have calls re-routed or unplug any phones in the room.
- Locate restrooms.
- Check seating and rearrange if necessary.
- Set up your visual aids; make sure they can be seen from every seat.
- Make sure you can be heard from the back of the room.
- Tape wires down if needed.
- Check the room lighting.
- Do body warm-ups, stretches, relaxation exercises.
- Check your appearance; make any adjustments.
- Greet your audience members as they arrive.

- If other speakers are presenting before you, be sure to listen to their presentations. You can then make connections to their content, examples, etc., and your material.
- Be gracious and authentic – on and off the stage.

Chapter 18

Conquering Stage Fright: Turn Fear Into Excitement

"Raise your level of performance to meet your expectations. Expect the best of yourself, and then do what is necessary to make it a reality." ~Ralph Marston, author

Have you heard that death and public speaking are two of Americans' biggest fears?

So, what do you do when your career depends on you mastering the art of delivering presentations?

No matter how cleverly you construct a presentation, no matter how eye-catching your slides, how insightful your anecdotes, none of it will do you any good if you walk out onto the stage, knees knocking, and freeze!

Whether this is your first presentation, or your hundredth, almost everyone suffers from some level of stage fright or performance anxiety. Actors and singers suffer from the same feelings, and many say they never get over them.

Carly Simon and Barbra Streisand for years refused to tour due to their incapacitating stage fright. Another mega-talented Grammy® Award-winning artist, Taylor Swift, also gets stage fright before performing in front of thousands. She uses positive self-talk to control these feelings -- literally talking to herself in front of a mirror to calm herself down before going on stage to perform. Swift repeatedly tells herself that she is "going to be OK." Given her sold-out performances, I'm guessing this technique worked and that she was more than OK.

There's no need to put yourself through hours, days, or even weeks of terror anticipating a presentation. Use the time to prepare and practice so you truly own the material. Nothing will replace that! At that point, what is the worst that can happen?

Identify your fears. Most anxious speakers fall prey to one or more of these six common fears:

- **Fear of your mind going blank.** This can and does happen. Barbra Streisand forgot the words to one of her songs mid concert, and refused to appear onstage again for many years. But a blank mind doesn't have to spell disaster for your presentation.

  Thorough practice really does limit the possibility of your mind going blank. That's why I don't suggest that you memorize your material when you practice. Say it differently each time -- that way you "own" the flow and content and don't get thrown by questions or a momentary blank mind.

  But if it happens, pause, look at your notes to pick up again where you left off, or move on to your next thought. Don't be afraid to use your notes to get back on track. If you later make a mistake, correct it if it's important, or let it slide if unimportant.

- **Fear of looking nervous, having shaky hands, sweating and being flushed.** Yes, this can be embarrassing, but there are many techniques to help you control these symptoms. I still get the last-minute jitters before addressing an audience. (I'll go into greater detail later in this chapter.) You need never call attention to physical symptoms of anxiety. If you keep your focus on the audience and not on yourself, the symptoms will dissipate.

- **Fear that someone will challenge you and you won't know the answer.** Don't lose sleep over this one because it's OK to not know every answer to a question. Honest! Just remember: NEVER lie. Of course, you should always anticipate (and prepare responses to) questions that may be asked. See Chapter 19 for more details. Along with preparing for the audience's questions, practice these statements: "I don't have the answer to that; let me research it and get back to you." Or, "Let's see if anyone in the audience has that information?"

- **Fear the audience won't think you know enough to be an expert,** and have no business acting like one. If you have backed up your material with facts and figures, and anecdotes to illustrate your points, this shouldn't be a problem. Do your homework!

- **Fear of a bad presentation ruining your reputation.** This is a legitimate fear, particularly if you are presenting to senior management. If you haven't prepared thoroughly, including taking time to know your audience, a bad presentation may damage your reputation. If you've done the upfront preparation and still floundered a bit when presenting live, chances are it wasn't as bad as you think. If you do receive negative evaluations or bad feedback from participants or the client stakeholder, address this concern head on. If you show high integrity to satisfy the client and practice to eliminate any similar, future errors, this one blemish probably will not ruin your reputation.

- **Fear of making a fool of yourself and being judged or ridiculed.** Of course, this is the biggie that probably underlies all the others. If you're well prepared and have practiced enough, everything should go smoothly. It's important that the audience feels your enthusiasm for your subject, even if you've made some mistakes or have lost your place. A sincere presenter doing his or her best, who's obviously well prepared and interested in the audience, will not be judged harshly. So, relax.

Presentation Tip: Remember to ask yourself, "What is the worst that can happen?" Then, ask, "What is the reality of that happening?" Then, prepare and practice so it won't!

Once you've identified your fears, begin working to manage them. First, accept that stage fright is a normal feeling, experienced by most people. Just view it as excitement. After all, the symptoms are similar. Next, observe how other speakers handle their anxiety. Ask what they do to relax before a presentation. Perhaps you've noticed speakers doing breathing exercises, or shoulder and head rolls before their presentations. Many speakers have brief exercise routines that help them relax. Others use self-talk -- like Taylor Swift does -- to turn the fear into excitement.

Here are several time-tested methods for beating stage fright...

Self-Talk Builds Self-Esteem.

Your internal conversations build or destroy your self-image. If you can regulate your self-talk to upgrade your self-image, you can convince yourself of almost anything. If you walk into a presentation believing you are going to fail, you probably will. Positive self-talk is an effective means of controlling stage fright. The goal is to be inwardly cocky and outwardly confident. No one wants to see an uptight, nervous speaker.

I frequently use a self-talk mantra: "I'm glad I'm here. I'm glad you're here. I know that I know." I repeat this mantra over and over to myself until I am relaxed. The message you are sending to yourself is one of joy and ease. It expresses your pleasure in being there to present. It says, "I'm thinking about you," and communicates that you have taken the time and effort to prepare a presentation worth giving and hearing.

Visualize Success.

Picture yourself in front of the audience. You are composed, confident, and in control. In your mind's eye, you watch yourself as you successfully reach out to the attendees and deliver an audience-centered presentation. You may want to include a positive response by the audience. Standing ovation, anyone?

By picturing yourself in a successful situation, you are able to give yourself the confidence you need to achieve your goal. Visualization techniques are time tested and proven successful by everyone from politicians to Olympic athletes.

Stay in Control.

There are many things you can do to ensure a successful presentation. Doing them will take a load off your mind, and make you that much more comfortable.

- **Arrive early.** This gives you a chance to relax, talk to audience members, survey your surroundings, make a trip to the restroom, organize your thoughts, and check the facilities – as well as any equipment you may be using. Rushing in at the last minute does you a disservice and amps up the anxiety. We all need the time to mentally prepare ourselves for the event at hand.

- **Eat lightly.** Avoid having a heavy meal right before you present. This also means no alcohol or dairy products (they create dry mouth), and nothing that might cause your stomach to be upset. Bananas are a good choice, they are light and filling – and the potassium will give you necessary energy. Avoid taking medications that might make you drowsy. You don't want to appear tired during your presentation.

- **Use humor in your presentation to help release endorphins.** Laughter is a great tension reliever. This helps you and your audience members relax.

- **Use interactive techniques.** Plan to ask audience members a question and get them to raise their hands. Or, have them brainstorm, or talk to a partner, or do any other interactive activities you can imagine. This will take some of the focus away from you, and put it onto them. You can use these moments to take a deep breath and relax.

At one presentation that I attended, the speaker had the entire audience learn a goofy little dance. We were all laughing and by the time we sat down, we were so relaxed and in such a good mood, that the speaker could have done no wrong!

This probably won't work at a board presentation, but getting the audience involved does help. Even some board members like to have fun.

> **Presentation Tip:** Before hitting the "stage," do some gentle stretches, toe touches, head/neck rolls, shoulder rolls and the like. They will loosen you up and let some of that tension go.

Another technique is called **"power posing."** Stand, walk for two minutes, making your body as large as possible. Swing your arms, take big steps. Do this in the hallways, restroom, etc.

If you are seated at a dais or table in the room, and waiting to present, do some **deep breathing** right at the table and extend your body. Both of the following deep breathing exercises help slow your heartbeat. As you do these breathing techniques, you also slow down the adrenaline surge that's making you tense.

Deep breathing I: Take a deep breath in through your nose and tighten everything in your body, from your head, neck, shoulder, hands, fingers, legs and toes. Hold the breath for six seconds, then slowly let go of the tension in your body as you exhale through your mouth to a count of 10.

Deep breathing II: Take a deep breath and clasp your hands together. Hold your breath as you squeeze your palms together tightly. Let go of your hands and exhale at the same time.

Power Posing

Got more stage fright symptoms?
I've got the solutions!

	Dos	Don'ts
For dry mouth	• Lightly coat your teeth with petroleum jelly; it will stop your lips from sticking to your teeth • Lightly bite the tip of your tongue (this helps you to salivate) • Drink room temperature or warm water (with lemon, if available)	• No milk products, soda, alcoholic beverages, caffeine, sugar
For sweaty hands/body	• Use talcum powder or corn starch • Carry a handkerchief	
If your voice is shaky	• Project your voice to the back row of the audience	• Avoid being soft spoken
If your hands are shaky	• Use deliberate gestures, that are controlled	• Don't over gesture • Don't hold anything that makes the shaking noticeable
If your legs are shaky or your knees are knocking:	• Move; take two to three steps	• Don't lock your knees together
If your heartbeat is rapid	• Do some deep breathing	• Avoid caffeine

A New Method for Beating Stage Fright?

There's no one method of controlling stage fright that works for everyone; the only important thing is what works for you. If trying to calm down isn't helping, researchers at Harvard Business School have come up with a new strategy to manage anxiety: getting excited!

According to their research (published in the *Journal of Experimental Psychology*), this is effective because it forces people to think about the positives, rather than their fears.

Study author Alison Wood Brooks, an assistant professor of business administration, said, "People have a very strong intuition that trying to calm down is the best way to cope with their anxiety, but that can be very difficult and ineffective. When people feel anxious and try to calm down, they are thinking about all the things that could go badly. When they are excited, they are thinking about how things could go well."

Makes sense to me. I know that when I get excited about something, there's a bit of an adrenaline rush that feels similar to anxiety, only it's pleasurable, not debilitating. Is it possible that the feeling of excitement can simply overshadow the feeling of fear? According to the study's researchers, it might be easier for people to view anxiety as excitement since both are states of high arousal.

One of the study's experiments involved 140 people who were asked to write a persuasive public speech on a specific topic. In a (successful) attempt to increase participants' anxiety, their speeches were videotaped. They were told that their performances would be later judged by a committee.

Here's the fascinating part: Each participant was advised to say, either, "I am excited" or "I am calm" before delivering their speeches. According to the study results, participants who used the phrase "I am excited" gave lengthier and more compelling speeches than those who used "I am calm." They were also judged as more effective and relaxed.

"The way we talk about our feelings has a strong influence on how we actually feel," Brooks said. "Even if they don't believe it at first, saying, 'I'm excited' out loud increases authentic feelings of excitement."

So, apparently, excited is the new relaxed.

If all else fails, keep in mind that in every presentation, there are three components: you (the speaker), the speech material (content), and the audience.

Note where the arrows are pointing. You, the speaker, need to be focused on the material and the audience. You need to make sure that the audience is getting the message.

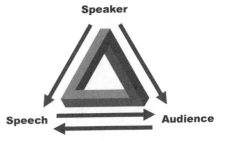

Where are the arrows pointing when you are nervous? Back at you. You are thinking one of three things:

- I should have said ...
- He doesn't like me
- I forgot to say ...

I, I, I. Wrong!

Stay focused on the audience. Ensure that they are connecting with the information. Forget about yourself.

Unless you are a rock star, CEO, star athlete, etc. – the audience members came to get information that would benefit them.

Get your ego out of the way!

Come with an attitude of service, not ego. By keeping this in mind (and having done your preparation and practice), you will have no trouble turning your stage fright symptoms into excitement!

Just realize that you aren't nervous. You are excited.

Presentation Tip: The more you speak in front of others, the more comfortable with it you'll become. The more you practice, the better speaker you will become. Period. There's no other magic to it.

Chapter 19
Handling the Q & A

"Before I refuse to take your questions, I have an opening statement." ~ Ronald Reagan

The last "official" chapter in this book is about handling questions. In some ways, it is one of the most important chapters.

I've heard really good presentations that ultimately failed due to the Q & A session. The speakers never anticipated what the questions would be, so they weren't prepared to go "deeper" than the PowerPoint slides. They were caught short.

Unfortunately, this is the last thing that the audience members will remember. So, the actual presentation was forgotten.

Bottom line: It's important to spend time planning, preparing and practicing for the Q & A.

You may ask why it's even important to take questions when you are presenting. After all, they do make a presentation so much more complicated. They eat into your time, and there's always the chance that someone in your audience will be hostile, show you up, monopolize the floor, or ask questions you just can't answer.

Opening yourself up to questions can be daunting, to say the least. The dreaded Q & A, however, is really a terrific opportunity for you to further clarify your ideas.

And even if it *is* true, you certainly don't want to give the audience the impression you're relieved that you survived the presentation and you can't wait to get away.

Giving your audience members the freedom to ask questions allows them to self-customize the message by getting what they want from you, the speaker. Questions turn a monologue into a dialogue, increase the level of audience connection and engagement, and, if handled well, increase audience satisfaction.

The secret to mastering the Q & A is no secret at all. It's the same thing I've been talking about throughout this book: Preparation!

Audience questions may be totally spontaneous, but the speaker's handling of them should not be.

Presentation Tip: With careful thought, most questions can be anticipated and prepared for.

Of course, there might be the odd, out-of-left-field query nobody could have anticipated, but those are usually the exception, not the rule.

Part of your presentation prep includes finding out as much as possible about your audience members. Armed with this knowledge, sit down and consider your topic from their point of view.

- Try to understand the perspective of your audience members -- what their needs are, what they are likely to be concerned or skeptical about. You should be able to identify their most likely questions.
- Do at least one practice session in front of people similar to your audience, and make note of their questions.
- Make a list of these questions, add any others you can think of, and prepare short, concise answers. Rehearse your answers.

Presentation Tip: If some of the likely questions will be confrontational, awkward, or about difficult things, consider *pre-empting* them.

Pre-empting questions involves bringing up an issue *before* someone asks you about it. This is important for questions that might put you at some sort of disadvantage. Sure, you'd rather leave that potential hot-potato out of your presentation entirely, but if you are taking questions, that might not be possible. Taking the initiative and bringing it up yourself puts you in the power position.

Here's an example: "Now, I know some of you are going to want to know how we went so far over budget. So, before you ask, my team is preparing a full report on what happened that will be in your in-boxes by the end of the week."

This pre-emptive approach may sound unwise if the issue is difficult. After all, there's always a chance no one will ask. But that's not a risk worth taking. Left to chance, the awkward matter could be raised in a contentious or hostile way. It could come at a particularly disruptive point in your presentation. When you bring it up yourself, you can craft the wording and speak to the matter on your terms, at your timing.

It's like that timeless sports expression, "The best defense is a good offense."

Presentation Bonus: Pre-empting potentially troublesome questions boosts your credibility. Even if the answers you give aren't wholly satisfactory, you get points for being open and not attempting to avoid trouble, hide from issues, or be evasive.

Presentation Pitfall: "That's a good question." Although intended to encourage questions, this common, overused response seems to have the opposite effect!

As some questions are labeled "good question" or "interesting question," audience members notice that their questions are being judged. The speaker is showing a preference for some questions over others. He or she seems pleased by certain questions, whereas others are merely answered without a word.

As this becomes apparent, audience members who are unsure about asking a question remain silent. ("What if my question is stupid?") The speaker was hoping to encourage more questions, but now receives even fewer.

Don't avoid this problem by complimenting all questions; it will very quickly sound ridiculous and you will lose credibility. You can thank people for their questions, just be sure not to rate or compliment them.

Keep Everyone in the Loop

Is there anything more frustrating than sitting toward the back or side of an audience, unable to hear the questions coming from people in front of you or on the other side of the room?

It's doubly frustrating when the speaker gives an answer that makes no sense, because you had no idea what was asked.

There are two main ways to make sure everyone knows what has been asked:

- Paraphrase the question. *"You are asking, 'How long*

do we plan to go before we launch a second generation device?"'

- Answer in a full sentence. It's not necessary to repeat a question if your answer contains the question. If you are asked, for example, how much is left in a budget, don't just give a number ($10,000). Answer in a full sentence: *"There is $10,000 dollars left in the budget."* Then, when audience members hear the answer, they will know what the question was.

Keep it Concise

Long answers discourage further questions. Rambling on at the end of a presentation can really diffuse the power of your concise, well-thought-out content already provided. If you respond to every question with a 10-minute lecture, no one will risk setting you off again by asking another question. They'll think: "I'll just keep my mouth shut or we'll be here all night!" So, keep your answers concise, no matter how many additional things you could say.

If they want more, they will ask. Avoid saying, "Did I answer your question?" Instead, say, "What other questions do you have about this?" This ensures they don't feel put on the spot.

Presentation Pitfall: Faking an answer is a huge no-no. Even if you've done your best to prepare for every possible question, you may find yourself unable to answer one. When this happens, never make up an answer — ever! It's entirely possible the person asking the question knows the answer, but wants to hear your opinion. Or, someone else in the audience knows the answer. You will be labeled a fraud immediately. People *will* talk, and your hard-won credibility will be out the window.

It's acceptable to say that you don't know the answer to a question — as long as you help the questioner get an answer. We are only human, after all. Even the top experts in any field don't always know everything. It's impossible.

The classic (and still appropriate) answer is: "I don't know the answer to that, but I'll find out and get back to you." Then, make sure you *do* get back to the person. He or she probably won't expect you to, so your effort will score points. If you have no intention to get back to the person, but know where he or she can get the answer, say, "I'm not sure of that answer, but if you call human resources, they will have the correct information."

You might also call on someone specific in the audience who might know, or open it up to the whole audience to answer. If you call on a specific person, make sure to say that person's name and *repeat the question.* If you don't repeat it, and he or she wasn't paying attention ... *awkward!*

Handling Hostile Questions and Challenges

How do you handle hostile questions and other challenging audience behaviors? Calmly and professionally.

Your skill disarming verbal attacks reflects your credibility and the impression your audience has of you and your presentation.

Diffuse hostile questioners by remembering the acronym **VIPP:**

V – Let them Vent. We all have a strong need to be heard, so listen!

I – *I hear what you're saying.* Paraphrase what they said and their feelings (but be careful not to sound condescending): "Your delivery was quite late; I understand why you are frustrated."

P – *Ask Probing questions* to determine the real issues. Angry people frequently make general condemnations of what's being proposed, when their real reason for being upset might be something else entirely. You need to get them to be more specific. "What part of the plan are you most concerned about?"

P – Use a *Problem*-solving statement. "Now that I
understand the problem, here is my response." Or, "Let's
look into it further after this presentation has concluded."
Agree that what the person specified is a legitimate concern,
and promise to problem-solve. Or disagree, after finding
something you can agree with. "I agree that it's a big
number, but it's a worthwhile investment."

The VIPP approach shows that you value the questioner's
thoughts and feelings. The audience will respect you, and
you'll diffuse the hostility at the same time. In a large group,
you can agree to discuss the situation offline with those who
are involved.

> **Presentation Tip:** Never allow yourself to engage in an
> argument with an audience member. Always look to diffuse
> a situation, rather than allow it to escalate.

Other techniques to effectively handle the Q & A include:

1) Leave your "but" out of an argument. "Yes. That
   happened, and (not but) here's what we're doing
   about it."

2) When someone says, "Your information isn't correct,"
   respond: "Where did your information come from?"

3) Look at the questioner while paraphrasing the question,
   but *look at the entire audience* when answering. Think
   inclusive, not exclusive.

4) Call on experts in the audience when appropriate, but
   take back control after they respond.

5) Inform those with multiple questions not relevant to the
   entire group, or relevant at all, that you'll respond
   either at the end of the session or later, by e-mail or
   phone.

6) Don't let a stage hog take control.

7) End the question-and-answer period with a strong
   closing remark.

If you are going to take questions, you'll need to know two
more things:

- How to encourage questions
- How to control questions

How to Encourage Questions

Open up the Q&A by asking, "What questions do you have?"
or, "Who would like to ask the first question?"

Be sure to wait up to 10 seconds before commenting. People
need time to think about the questions they may want to
ask. In some groups, no one will raise a hand and go first, so
you'll have to make the first move.

Do this by saying, "A question I am usually asked is ..." or,
"a question I first had ..." That should encourage others to
speak up, after you've answered your own question.

- If the person says, "I don't agree," respond, "What
  about it don't you agree with?" You can always do
  what politicians do – spin your answer: "What you
  really want to be asking is..."

If the decision maker is asking the question, always take the
time to answer it. But don't dwell on it; keep it moving.

> **Presentation Tip:** After responding to a challenge, a hostile
> question, or a topic you'd just as soon move away from,
> don't say, "Did that answer your question?" That can reopen
> the discussion — the opposite of what you want.

Presence Trumps Answers

Long after people forget your answers — or lack thereof —

they remember how you responded to tough questions and challenges. They remember your presence, your leadership qualities, and the overall presentation.

If you stayed calm, didn't panic or start babbling at top speed, didn't become defensive or evasive, and treated the audience members politely, your image will be that of a confident and competent presenter.

More Q&A Tips

Aside from, "Never let them see you sweat."...

Let audience members know (in your introduction during your preview) when you'll be taking questions. You have several options:

- Ask them to write their questions down to save for the end.
- Invite them to ask throughout your presentation.

- Inform them there will be specific breaking points during the presentation for questions.

Create a more conversational, informal atmosphere by getting closer to the audience.

- Step out from behind the lectern or table; even sit down at the table if the audience will still be able to see you.
- Some speakers like to take questions standing right in the audience. If the room setup is appropriate and you feel comfortable, it is acceptable to run the Q & A session this way.
- Pay close attention to your own body language, keeping it open and relaxed. Avoid rolling your eyes, sighing, or cleaning up your notes.
- You could use the technique of having audience members text you questions or put questions on cards and hand them in.
- "Bribing" the audience with candy, books, etc., often

encourages people to participate.
- You can ask people to turn to the person next to them and have the two of them come up with questions.

How to Control the Timing of the Q & A

As the presenter, it is up to you to control when you will take questions. Here are five tips:

- If you are giving a training session or a sales presentation, it makes sense to take questions during your presentation. If someone asks a question you'll be covering later, you can say so, or answer the question and then get back on track.
- Avoid lengthy responses to questions that disrupt your train of thought and the audience's concentration.
- You can set aside question-and-answer periods for specified times during a presentation. Let the audience know this as part of the preview. This gives your audience members the chance to formulate their questions while you present.
- You can also ask the audience to wait until the end before asking questions.
- If you are presenting to leadership teams, be prepared to be interrupted throughout your presentation. So, plan your presentation accordingly.

Never end with the Q & A session. End with a strong conclusion.

When there are no more questions, or your time is up, take one more opportunity to leave a positive impression. Return to the central theme, revert to your closing statement, or talk about next steps. Your closing should not be lengthy, but wrap things up neatly.

An example might be: "We've learned how and why a formal coaching program can build stronger, more motivated teams and individuals, and help our sales force meet and exceed their quotas every month. Let's take the steps to implement this program today."

Key Takeaways

- A good presentation will go down the tubes if the Q&A session is handled poorly.
- Anticipate – what questions will they ask – then, prepare your answers.
- Keep your answers brief. Long answers discourage more questions. If they want more, they will ask.
- When asked a question...
    - ✓ avoid complimenting
    - ✓ be sure to paraphrase or include the question as part of your answer
- If you are challenged, use the VIPP formula. Never get defensive or argumentative.
- Always end the Q&A session on a positive note.

Chapter 20
Final Thoughts

The ability to present your ideas clearly, concisely and confidently is critical for career success. You may only be presenting to one person, but that's still a presentation. Every successful professional needs to speak well.

Brilliant presentations are crafted from a thorough understanding of your subject matter, your audience's needs, and the step-by-step knowledge of how to make masterful presentations that inform and persuade.

Brilliant presenters are created by care, thoughtfulness, passion, and experience. Take the necessary steps to implement stronger presentation skills, and you'll reap the related career rewards.

If there's one final note I'd like to leave you with, it's to remember that practice makes polished. Practice makes professional ... and, practice makes permanent!

For more information about BRODY's
programs and services, contact:
115 West Avenue, Suite 114
Jenkintown, PA 19046
215-886-1688; info@BrodyPro.com
www.BrodyPro.com

Index